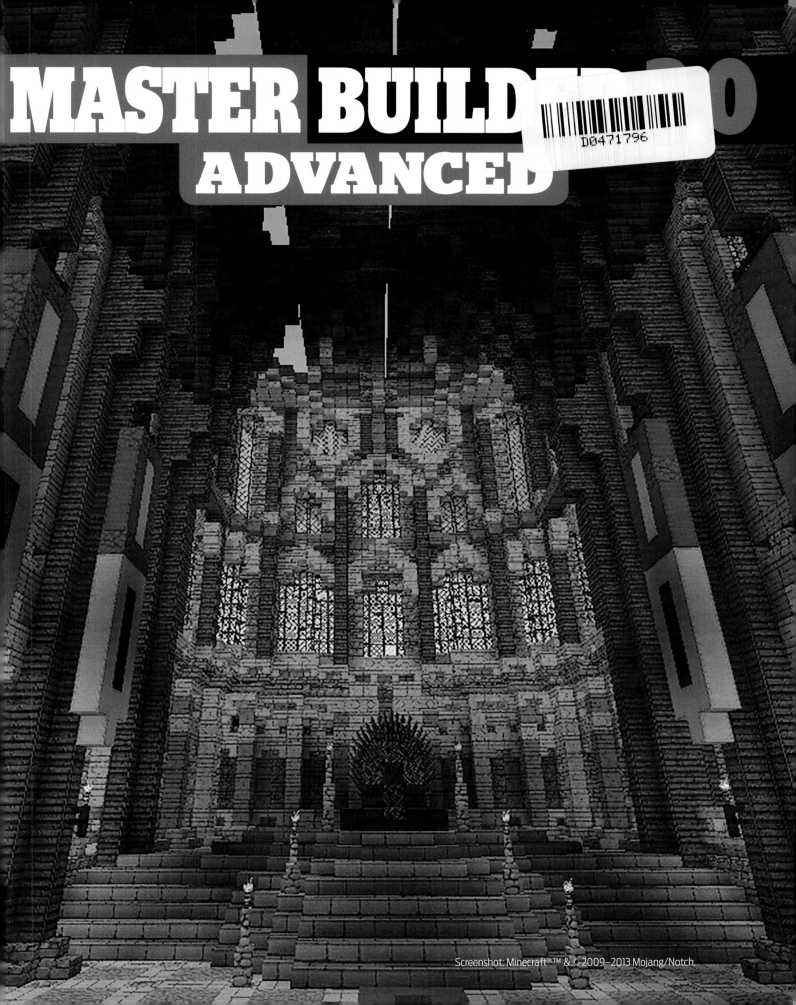

# MASTER BUILDER PRO
## ADVANCED

**MASTER BUILDER 3.0 ADVANCED**

This book is available in quantity at special discounts for your group or organization.
For further information, contact:

**Triumph Books LLC**
814 North Franklin Street
Chicago, Illinois 60610
Phone: (312) 337-0747
www.triumphbooks.com

Printed in U.S.A.
ISBN: 978-1-62937-093-4

**Content packaged by Mojo Media, Inc.**
Joe Funk: Editor
Jason Hinman: Creative Director
Trevor Talley: Writer

# Contents

# Introduction

These are exciting days for Minecraft.

We are about to see what happens when the world's biggest software company gets its hands on the world's biggest video game. $2.5 billion is the figure that Microsoft, the company that brought about computing as we know it today, thinks that our favorite little blocky builder is worth, and what they paid to acquire it in 2014. As sales of Minecraft start to near the 70 million copies mark, as Minecraft makes the jump to new generation consoles marking 12 separate systems it can be played on, as the creator of the game buys a $70 million dollar house out from under the noses of the world's biggest popstars, that figure of $2.5 billion overshadows all others figures.

That's not just because it's the most anyone has ever paid to own a video game, it's because it's a number for the future. It's one of the most important companies in the world saying that they believe they can not only make $2.5 billion on Minecraft in the years to come, but that they will make more than $2.5 billion.

That, oh Crafters, is very good news for us that play this innocuous seeming building game. In fact, it's incredible news. Whatever your feelings on Notch no longer being at the helm of Minecraft (it seems like he just wanted a little privacy, and who can blame him), all fans of Minecraft should be happy with at least one thing:

**Minecraft is here to stay, and it's only going to get bigger.**

With that in mind, this is our new Minecraft book, and it is all about celebrating this game that has already taken over the minds and screens of the world, and which seems poised to become even more massive in the coming years.

Where our first two titles were all about learning the basics of the game and solidifying those lessons to become a highly skilled Crafter, Master Builder 3.0 Advanced is about learning what you can do with this game when you've mastered those basic lessons and are looking for the next big challenge, the next great Minecraft adventure.

That is what you will find in these pages: challenge and adventure.

We kicked open the door to the house of Minecraft in the last few books, we took our first steps in, we got comfortable, and now it's time to explore the rest of the rooms. It's time to go deeper into Minecraft, to not just learn how to be great at playing Minecraft, but to dive into every crevice of Minecraftian knowledge that there is in the world. And you probably already know, there is quite a lot of it out there to find. There are many rooms in the house that is Minecraft.

To begin our dive into the deep parts of the game, we're going to show you one of the secrets behind those eyeball-popping, gorgeous maps and Minecraft screenshots that draw so many people to this game and leave even grizzled Minecraft veterans shaking their heads in awe.

Then, we'll spend a bit of time online, showing you where you can go to expand your knowledge and become a true part of this community of over 100 million registered players, and to see what the unbelievable talent residing in that community has done with this game that's as much a creative medium as it is entertainment.

From there we'll show you how to customize Minecraft and turn it from cool-looking, if a little pixely, to downright gorgeous, and we'll show you how to do it in a way that makes your Minecraft world look as unique as the mind that created it.

Next we'll show you the way of the mini-game, a deceptive title for the myriad ways that fans just

like you have taken Minecraft and turned it into something entirely different, creating all new ways to play and amplifying the traditional modes so that they become epic. One in particular, UHC, we've given a whole chapter, because it is to Minecraft what chess is to board games—a game for experts and true competitors. Be warned though: after reading about these so called "mini" games, you may find yourself neglecting your regular world—they're just that good.

Then, it's 20 pages of exploring servers and mods, a pagebound trip through the other worlds that Minecraft can show you besides your standard vanilla game, including both those you can fire up alone or with a few friends and get lost in, and those that constantly thrive and bustle online with the living population of a decent sized town.

A quick stop to challenge your Crafting skills, to put you and your friends to the true Minecraft test and see who can triumph, is followed by our best gallery of Minecraft creations yet, complete with

classic, gorgeous edifices of the past few years and a slew of projects so new, they hadn't been out a week before we finished this book.

And then, a world exclusive: an inspiring personal chat with a bonafide Minecraft celebrity about his love for the game and how he managed to turn that into something that earns him a fine living.

Following our look into the life of TheDiamond-Minecart, we'll help you scratch that itch for more building, more survival and more, of course, crafting with another list of the best other games that relate to each of these subjects, each of which is worth dozens of hours of your time in its own right.

Finally, we've included a free excerpt from our book, *The Ultimate Guide to Mastering Circuit Power!: Minecraft®™ Redstone and the Keys to Supercharging Your Builds in Sandbox Games,* which is designed specifically to help players of all levels get past the hurdle of understanding this most complex of video game systems and become a true Minecraft engineer. When it comes to getting more out of this game, and diving deeper, nothing will change your Minecraft experience quite like learning the secrets of Redstone.

And that's what this book is all about, really-taking your interest and passion for Minecraft and turning it up a notch, making it fresh again and again, and showing you ways to keep doing so for a long, long time. As we wait to see what Microsoft and Mojang have in store for us, we, like many of you, are excited, but we're not nervous. Because we know that this game is already infinitely deep, that there is always another world to see, another mode to dominate, another castle to explore and another mine to dive into.

So turn the page, Crafter, and let's do just that. ◼

— **Trevor Talley, author
@defenderdefends**

# Software To Boost Your Builds

Here's a little secret about some of the amazing Minecraft builds and images you've seen: not all of them were actually made in normal Minecraft. GASP! Shocking right? It's a little weird to hear for the first time, but software outside of Minecraft itself is actually a pretty big part of the creation of many big or complicated Minecraft projects and screenshots.

MCEdit will load up your Minecraft world in a couple of different views, including a map and one that looks pretty much like the game, but which can be flown around and edited with almost no lag (delay).

Some folks are of a mind that Minecraft projects should be built by hand, block-by-block in the regular game, and that's totally fine, but there are others out there who see Minecraft as more of a creative medium than something that they want to toil at for weeks and weeks just to get a map done, and we think that's fine, too.

When it comes down to it, we think it doesn't really matter how an awesome map gets made or a screenshot gets taken, it only matters that it's amazing and that we get to see it and/or play around in it. Most of the time when you're in a map that used special software, you'll never know that it wasn't made the regular way, and in fact the ability to edit maps far more quickly and use special tools actually allows players to create types of maps that we would never see otherwise. For images, this is even more the case, as the programs that are out there to create Minecraft screenshots from a map are far, far more powerful and create much more gorgeous images than the game could ever create on its own.

If cutting down the amount of time it takes to create a building or making the most stunning screenshots possible is something that interests you, we definitely recommend checking out one of the following programs. And remember: you only have to use them as much or as little as you want, and the end result is what's most important, not the way you did it.

Oh, and all of these are totally free!

# MCEdit
**mcedit.net**

**What it is:** A very powerful, yet pretty easy to use program that edits Minecraft worlds outside of the game

MCEdit is definitely the most widely-used Minecraft program besides the game itself, and many, many of the most popular maps were at least partly created using this bad boy. Essentially every block you need to place can be placed with MCEdit, but it also can do special things that you normally couldn't do, such as get a detailed map of your world quickly, place multi-block pieces down at once and use tools to "erode" the landscape in natural-looking patterns (which keeps you from having to try and do that manually, a tricky business).

The best parts about MCEdit are that your maps load and can be flown around very smoothly and with little system lag, and that it is crazy easy to use for being so powerful. Definitely worth your time for big projects.

# VoxelSniper

**dev.bukkit.org/bukkit-plugins/voxelsniper**
**kraftzone.net/wiki/VoxelSniper**
**thevoxelbox.com**

**What it is:** An in-game editor and brush array that allows for editing a world at any distance and which features powerful terrain and object creation tools

Created by one of Minecraft's premier servers and builder communities, The Voxel Box, VoxelSniper is the in-game answer to MCEdit. Instead of loading your world up in software outside to edit, or having to build the regular way in-game, VoxelSniper allows you to add or remove blocks as far away as you can see in the game.

All you do is select the special "arrow" tool (to add) or the "gunpowder" tool (to delete), point at where you want to add or remove a block, and click, and it will do so!

Additionally, VoxelSniper comes with an array of "brushes" that will add or remove multiple blocks in specially designed patterns. You can set a brush size, then pick between brushes like the Erosion Brush, the Tree Brush, the Ring Brush and many many more, each of which places or removes blocks to create the effects that they're named after. The patterns these brushes make are very nicely designed and made specifically for Minecraft, so they end up having a great many uses in big creative worlds.

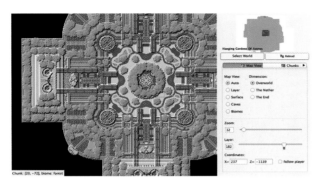

Renders in Chunky are set up by selecting portions of a build as seen from above (like it is here), and then adjusting the first person view.

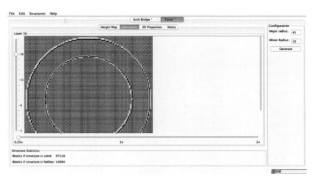

A view of Tectonicus, one of our Other Tools, which helps players to build certain shapes by giving them the design layer by layer.

# Chunky

**chunky.llbit.se**

**What it is:** An outside of game tool that creates images of a world that are not possible to render in regular Minecraft

Compared to the last two tools, Chunky is quite a bit more complicated to use, partially because the language it uses and the concepts it deals with are more about image rendering and creation than about playing Minecraft. That being said, many of the very best Minecraft screenshots are created with Chunky, and those looking to show off what they've built will find it invaluable to their efforts.

Basically what it does is load your world outside of Minecraft in an editor that shows you a visual map from the top down, allowing you to select the chunks of the map you would like in your image. You then create a "scene," which loads from the perspective of where your character was when you saved last, or you can place the view in a specific spot. You can then move the view around a little bit and tweak a wide array of settings to create exactly the image that you want before you render and save it.

You can get pretty insanely creative with this tool, even setting things like the height of the sun, the focus of the camera, the exposure amount and

more, and the images that result are often quite beautiful. They also, however, can take quite a while to both set up and to render, so it's not a tool for quick-shots, but instead for the ones you want to make perfect.

# Other Tools

The tools we've listed are just the most popular and powerful of many, many available tools. A few others to check out, if these ones piqued your interest, include:

- JourneyMap (mapping)
- Tectonicus (mapping)
- AMIDST (finds dungeons and villages)
- Minecraft X-Ray (can see through maps to find items and blocks)
- Minecraft Editor (map editor)
- Terrain Control (custom biome and land creation)
- MCDungeon (makes dungeons and "treasure hunts" in already created maps)
- NovaSkin (skin editor)
- MCSkinner (skin editor)
- Minecraft Texture Studio (create your own resource packs)
- INVedit (inventory editor)
- Mineways (export your world to a 3D printer)

Google | minecraft | 🔍     jason@intersectmedia.com ▾

Web   Videos   News   Images   Shopping   More ▾   Search tools      ⚙

About 130,000,000 results (0.17 seconds)

**Minecraft**
https://**minecraft**.net/ ▾ Minecraft ▾
**Minecraft** is a game about breaking and placing blocks. At first, people built structures to protect against nocturnal monsters, but as the game grew players ...

| | |
|---|---|
| **Download it here**<br>... the game, you can download the<br>stand-alone launcher for ... | **To Play The Demo**<br>Minecraft. Please log in or register for<br>a Mojang account to play ... |
| **Log in**<br>Minecraft is a game about placing<br>blocks to build anything you ... | **Store**<br>Minecraft is a game about placing<br>blocks to build anything you can ... |

More results from minecraft.net »

**In the news**
Play Info Quest II. You might learn something…
Mojang - 2 days ago
... on this entry are closed. Previous post: **Minecraft** 1.8.2-pre1 – Christmas Gift Edition.
Next post: **Minecraft** Skin Studio Encore now available!

Minecraft Creator's New $70m Beverly Hills Mansion, Rebuilt in Minecraft
GameSpot - 6 hours ago

Of Course Someone Made Notch's $70 Million Mansion In Minecraft
Kotaku - 1 day ago

More news for minecraft

**Minecraft - Wikipedia, the free encyclopedia**
en.wikipedia.org/wiki/**Minecraft** ▾ Wikipedia ▾
**Minecraft** is a sandbox independent video game originally created by Swedish programmer Markus "Notch" Persson and later developed and published by the ...

**Official Minecraft Wiki - The ultimate resource for all things ...**
**minecraft**.gamepedia.com/ ▾
Welcome to the **Minecraft** Wiki, a publicly accessible and editable wiki for information related to **Minecraft**. The wiki and its 3,620 articles and 10,213 files are ...

**Minecraft**
Video game

★★★★½ 4.5/5 - Google Play
★★★★½ 4.5/5 - Apple

Minecraft is a sandbox independent video game originally created by Swedish programmer Markus "Notch" Persson and later developed and published by the Swedish company Mojang since 2009. Wikipedia

**Initial release date:** May 17, 2009
**Developers:** 4J Studios, Mojang
**Designers:** Jens Bergensten, Markus Persson
**Awards:** VGX Award for Best Independent Game, BAFTA Games Special Award
**Platforms:** Android, PlayStation 3, PlayStation Vita, PlayStation 4, More
**Publishers:** Sony Computer Entertainment, Microsoft Studios, Mojang

**People also search for**     View 5+ more

|  |  |  |  |  |
|---|---|---|---|---|
| Terraria<br>2011 | Grand Theft<br>Auto V<br>2013 | Garry's Mod<br>2004 | World of<br>Warcraft<br>2004 | Counter-...<br>1999 |

Feedback

# Minecraft On The Web:
## Sites To Enhance Your Game

If you thought Minecraft's domination of your computation machine ended at the game itself, get ready to be awed at the ever-widening scope of this deceptively humble game. Minecraft has a massive online presence, with so very many websites dedicated to various aspects of the game that it feels like they're just about infinite.

Among those thousands and thousands and, yes, more thousands of sites are a few that have become an integral part of many players' Minecraft experience. Knowing which of these sites to go to and what they're good for can not only improve your skills at the game, it can also provide all new experiences. From watching the Let's Plays of YouTube where Minecraft celebrities film their exploits, to downloading the latest greatest maps off Planet Minecraft to chatting with fellow Crafters on the Forum and Reddit, it's a big, wide world of Minecraft out there on the Internet, and it's waiting for you just a few clicks away.

Here we'll introduce you to the best of the best of these many sundry sites to get you started on your WebCraft explorations.

# Planet Minecraft

**planetminecraft.com**

**Focus:** Downloading, showcasing and uploading maps, skins, texture packs and servers, plus a large forum

Planet Minecraft is by far the most important website to the Minecraft creator community. Though there are other sites (especially those of individual creators) where you can download maps, skins and texture packs to play with in your own Minecraft game, Planet Minecraft is far and away the biggest, best and most popular repository of everything downloadable for Minecraft.

Nearly all the big names are on here, from SethBling to disco to Circleight to carloooo and more, and pretty much every famous map or game type or construction type can be found in the databases of Planet Minecraft. Heck, some of the maps we feature in our books were found on PM!

Not only can you download projects here, you can interact with the people who do, commenting on their maps and giving "Diamonds" to vote on the best projects, and you can even upload your own works for free! Got something you want to show off? Put it up on Planet Minecraft, and if it's good, it's almost guaranteed to be seen by thousands of people.

PM is amazing, and with literally thousands of new projects up every month, it's a never-ending parade of new things to try out. Mini-games, adventure maps, Redstone tutorials, PVP arenas, and massive, amazing worlds to explore- it's all here!

A typical Minecraft Wiki page, this one detailing the basics of crafting in the game. Pages on the Wiki range from the very short (stubs on some items, for instance), and the quite long, such as this entry or the one on Redstone.

# The Minecraft Wiki

**minecraft.gamepedia.com**

**Focus:** Information on many aspects of the game

Where Planet Minecraft is all about adding to your game, the Minecraft Wiki is there to give you information that you need to play. While it can be disorganized and some entries aren't kept up to date or written as well as others, if you need to know something quickly about an item or a specific aspect of the game, the Minecraft Wiki is where you want to go. It has a pretty straightforward search feature that will quickly bring you to the page on, as an example, potions, giving you all of the recipes and a bit about the concepts behind the subject. There's a ton of info here, though it's pretty self-guided and can vary in quality from entry to entry.

What definitely is awesome about the Wiki, however, is that it keeps a detailed history of Minecraft, from the content of each update to information on the history of its creation. That stuff is pure gold if you're into Minecraft trivia, and it can be a lot of fun to explore the thousands of pages and become even more of a Minecraft expert.

If you feel up to the task and have a little free time, you can actually become a contributor to the Minecraft Wiki by making an account and going through a vetting process. Contributors have to prove themselves, but eventually you can put your Minecraft knowledge to use tackling the ever-growing, never finished pile of "Wanted Articles" and "Stubs" that the Wiki would like to see added. It's a pretty cool way to be a part of the Minecraft community, and the top contributors are highly respected among older Crafters. You'll get to be a part of important conversations about the game, and even see some of the Mojang guys on there sometimes!

◆ Community portal          🖩 Create an account          ❖ Style guide
🏛 Admin noticeboard        ↗ Help contents              ◔ Copyrights
📢 Wiki rules               ✎ How to help                ▽ General disclaimer
                           Recent changes • New pages • Missing pages

Welcome to the Minecraft Wiki, a publicly accessible and editable wiki for information related to *Minecraft*. The wiki and its 3,617 articles and 10,214 files are managed and maintained by 340 active contributors from the *Minecraft* community, along with the wiki's administration team. Anyone can contribute.

## About *Minecraft*

**MINECRAFT** is a sandbox construction game created by Mojang AB founder Markus Persson, and inspired by the *Infiniminer*, *Dwarf Fortress* and *Dungeon Keeper* games. Gameplay involves players interacting with the game world by placing and breaking various types of blocks in a three-dimensional environment. In this environment, players can build creative structures, creations, and artwork on multiplayer servers and singleplayer worlds across multiple game modes.

*Minecraft* is available to all players for €19.95 (US$26.95, £17.95). When purchased, singleplayer and multiplayer game modes can be played using the downloadable stand-alone launcher. *Minecraft* Classic is available to play for free. *Minecraft* development started around May 10, 2009, and pre-orders for the full game started being accepted on June 13, 2009. *Minecraft's* official release date was November 18, 2011. On September 20, 2014, *Minecraft* for the computer reached 17 million sales and became the best-selling PC game of all time.

On August 16, 2011, *Minecraft: Pocket Edition* was released for the Sony Xperia Play gaming smartphone. After its exclusivity with Sony expired, it was released for Android devices on October 7, 2011, and iOS devices on November 17, 2011 for US$6.99. On April 2, 2014, *Minecraft* was released for the Amazon Fire TV. It contains all the same features as the *Pocket Edition* as well as support for the Fire TV's controller.

On May 9, 2012, *Minecraft* was released for the Xbox 360 on Xbox Live Arcade for US$20, where it subsequently broke every previous sales record.

On February 11, 2013, *Minecraft: Pi Edition* was released for the Raspberry Pi. It is based on the *Pocket Edition* and is available for free at Mojang's dedicated blog. The *Pi Edition* is intended as an educational tool for novice programmers and users are encouraged to open and change the game's code using its API.

On December 17, 2013, *Minecraft* was released for the PlayStation 3 on the PlayStation Store for US$19.99. The release was almost identical to the Xbox 360 Edition and was developed in tandem with the Xbox 360 Edition from then on.

On June 26, 2014, the Xbox 360 & PlayStation 3 editions' sales passed the number of sales for the PC edition of *Minecraft*, leaving the *Minecraft* series having sold more than 54 million copies world-wide and become third best-selling video game of all time.

*Minecraft* was released for the PlayStation 4 on September 4, 2014, the Xbox One on September 5, 2014 and the PlayStation Vita on October 14, 2014.

On September 15, 2014, Mojang AB and all of its assets (including *Minecraft*) were purchased by Microsoft for US$2.5 billion.

On December 10, 2014, *Minecraft: Pocket Edition* was released for Windows Phone 8.1.

## Play it!

**Computer edition**

🖥

Game  1.8.1   Launcher  1.5.3

**Pocket Edition**

🤖 android    iOS    fireTV    ⊞

0.10.4      0.10.4    0.10.0    0.10.4

**Console Edition**              **Pi Edition**

Ⓧ Xbox 360   Ⓧ Xbox   PS3        🍓 raspberry

TU16         TU1      1.06        0.1.1

PS4          PS VITA

1.01         1.01

Purchase the computer edition! (Demo)
Purchase the Pocket Edition! Android • iOS • Amazon Fire TV • Windows Phone 8.1
Purchase the Console Edition! Xbox 360 (Demo) • Xbox One • PlayStation 3 (Demo) • PlayStation 4 (Demo) • PlayStation Vita (Demo)
Download the Raspberry Pi Edition!

## Gameplay

Explanation of the various game modes and features used in *Minecraft*.

**Game modes**
- Survival
- Creative
- Hardcore
- Adventure
- Spectator
- Demo

**Recipes**
- Crafting
- Smelting
- Brewing

**Tutorials**
- New player
- General
- Mining
- Item farming

- Mob farming
- Enchanting & smelting
- Mechanism
- Technical

## Popular and useful pages

**Achievements**
  Information on achievements that can be collected in *Minecraft*.
**Blocks**
  Detailed information on the various blocks available in *Minecraft*.
**Items**
  Detailed information on the various items available in *Minecraft*.
**Biomes**
  Information about all biomes in *Minecraft*.
**Enchanting**
  Information about enchanting.
**Mobs**
  Information about the various friendly and non-friendly creatures found in *Minecraft*.
**Trading**
  Detailed information about villager trading.
**Redstone circuits**
  Information about redstone circuits.
**Resource packs**
  Various resource packs that alter the look and feel of the game.
**Modifications**
  Various modifications that alter the gameplay.

## News and events

**News**

**October 14, 2014**
  *Minecraft*: PlayStation Vita Edition was released.
**September 15, 2014**
  *Minecraft* and Mojang were bought by Microsoft.
**September 5, 2014**
  *Minecraft*: Xbox One Edition was released.
**September 4, 2014**
  *Minecraft*: PlayStation 4 Edition was released.
**August 1, 2014**
  *Minecraft* End-User License Agreement started to be enforced on all servers.

**Recent updates**

**November 24, 2014**
  *Minecraft* 1.8.1 released.
**November 18, 2014**
  *Minecraft* 0.10.0 released for the Pocket Edition.
**September 2, 2014**
  *Minecraft* 1.8 released.
**July 10, 2014**
  *Minecraft* Alpha 0.9.0 released for the Pocket Edition.
**June 26, 2014**
  *Minecraft* 1.7.10 released.

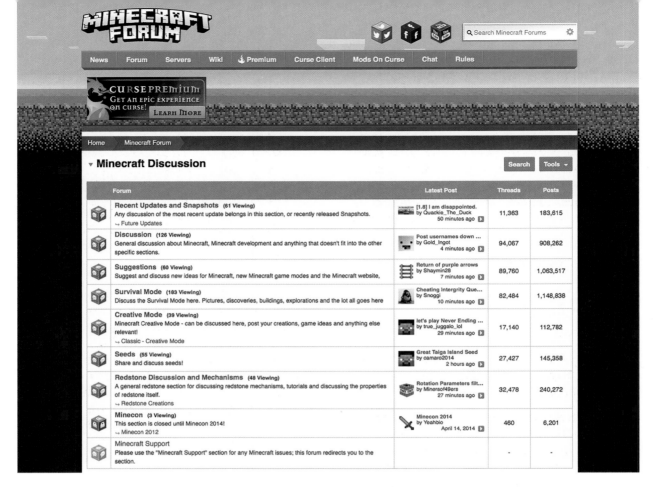

# Minecraft Forum

**minecraftforum.net**

**Focus:** Talking with others about all aspects of the game, as well as finding new maps, mods and more

The number one website for Crafters to gather and talk about Minecraft is the Minecraft Forum. Here anyone can make an account and chat with other Minecrafters about whatever they like, whether that's finding a new server, showing off screenshots, talking strategy or even chatting about other things that aren't Minecraft.

If you have a question about Minecraft, want to show something off that you did or want to find a new server to play on or new people to play with, the Minecraft Forum should be your first stop. Chances are, whatever your question or need, someone else has either asked the same question or can help you out quickly.

It's also common practice for most big mods, shaders, servers and some maps to have a page on here where their creators post information and the latest downloads for their creations. While Planet Minecraft has a lot of this stuff, the Forum usually has the most up-to-date version and a lot more info, and you'll find yourself going back and forth between the two sites a lot if you get into downloading add-ons for your game.

One thing to note about the forums: while they are heavily moderated, anyone can get on here, so be careful with what you post and who you talk to if you're still a young Crafter. Of course, most people on the Forum are super nice and happy to help you get better at the game, so don't worry too much, just keep your eye out for bad eggs.

**And always remember:** be nice and don't spam!

# YouTube

**youtube.com**

**Focus:** Let's Play videos of Minecrafters recording their gameplay, lists of great mods and maps, and tutorials for most things you'd want to try

The three previously mentioned sites are the biggest and best out there when it comes to Minecraft-specific content, but YouTube may be the most important Minecraft site when it comes to spreading and teaching the game. This is because in recent years gamers have taken to recording themselves playing games, especially Minecraft, and have uploaded videos of themselves doing so to the site.

Nowadays, it's one of the most popular topics on YouTube, and many folks have actually become Minecraft celebrities that make a living posting hilarious, insightful and downright entertaining Minecraft videos on the website.

Some of the biggest names include the Mindcrack group (Guude, SethBling, Nebris et al.), SkyDoesMinecraft, CaptainSparklez, stampylonghead, SSundee, TheDiamondMinecart

Even your trusty author has his own YouTube channel under the name DEFENDERPLAYSGAMES (note, channel meant for mature audiences).

and the ever popular Yogscast. Many of these folks have been on here a very long time and have millions of subscribers, not to mention videos that can rack up hundreds of thousands or even millions of views each. They typically are very entertaining, having refined their, *ahem*, Craft for years and over thousands of videos, and each one has a massive following that they interact with regularly. If you've never seen a Minecraft Let's Play, we suggest checking out Mindcrack's UHC videos, one of Yogscasts' series or one of the many, many Minecraft music videos out there to start off.

In addition to the entertainment value, YouTube is ideal for showing players how various things work in the game. Can't figure out how to make a Redstone gate, or curious what a certain mod does? Search for it on YouTube! We can absolutely guarantee someone has explained it very well on there, if not many someones.

If you like the idea of using YouTube for Minecraft, you can actually join yourself and start uploading your very own videos! You'll need some special software and a microphone, but it's pretty simple to do when you get it set up. And, not surprisingly, you can find out how to do all that set up on YouTube itself.

## Modloader Sites

**files.minecraftforge.net**
**feed-the-beast.com**
**technicpack.net**

**Focus:** Getting you those sweet, sweet mods and keeping you up to date with the modding community

Most major mods for Minecraft have a specific forum page dedicated to them, as mentioned, but the primary way most mods are announced and accessed is through a modloader page.

Forge is more about getting the actual loader itself, which is slightly complex, but the site contains good and easy walkthroughs to get you through it.

Feed the Beast and Technic, on the other hand, are pretty slick and actually have the mods accessible through the loaders themselves, meaning you don't have to do much except get the modloader downloaded from the website. Those last two especially are great for learning about new mods and reading the information about them, as they will give pretty detailed accounts and post fairly often (Technic most of all, perhaps).

There are other mod sites out there as well, so do a little exploring and see if you find one you really like!

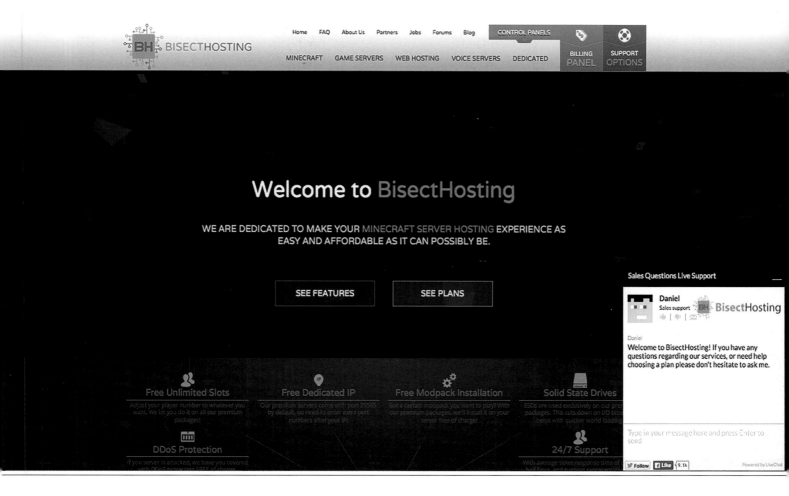

# Server Hosting Sites
## Many, many out there!

**Focus:** Sites that you can pay to host a private or public Minecraft server

If you play Minecraft on the PC, chances are you've thought about how cool it would be to be able to play with your friends on your own server. While you can always play a LAN game with friends, or get on a public server, if you want to play on a private world with people online, you either have to have your own dedicated server running or know someone who does.

Setting up a server is totally do-able, but it takes a lot of time and effort, and a lot can go wrong. Try and add something like mods or big maps in

there, and you'll quickly run into trouble. Typically people need an entire computer dedicated to running the server, plus a lot of expertise on server upkeep.

That's where server hosting sites come in: you just pay them a monthly fee, and they do the work and set up a server for you. There are a ton of options out there when it comes to pricing and what you get for your dollar, including hosts that will add mods for you, servers that allow many people to join at once and much more.

It's not something all players will want to do, but there really is something special about getting your own permanent game going with friends from all over the world, so if that sounds fun, definitely check out server hosting sites online.

# Skins, Resource Packs And Shaders:
## Making Your Minecraft Pretty

Minecraft is rather unique among games- this is something all players know. One way that it is unique that can sometimes go overlooked, however, is that Minecraft's structure of being mostly blocks with textures on them allows the look of Minecraft to be customized to a degree that few other games have ever seen. Because players and creative folk out in the world can basically take that blocky structure and create their own textures to lay over it, the exact same world and characters can be changed in nearly infinite ways to look differently, making for perhaps the most customizable visuals in any game ever created.

There are three basic components to Minecraft's visuals that can be customized: skins, texture or "resource" packs, and the trickier, but oh so awesome shaders. If you're looking to pretty up your Minecraft game and create an entirely unique look that can sometimes change even a standard Minecraft landscape into something worthy of a million screenshots, here's how you do that.

## Skins:
### Changing Your Character's Look

By far the easiest facet of your Minecraft visuals to give a facelift to is literally the face (and body) of your Minecraft character. Ole Steve, your standard Minecraft character model, is great and all, but at some point when playing online it gets pretty boring to look like every other schmoe out there. That's when it's time to change your Minecraft skin, and doing so is very, very easy.

**How to Change**
PC/Mac- Changing your skin on the PC or Mac versions of the games is actually done online through the official Minecraft website. Just head over to minecraft.net and click on the "Profile"

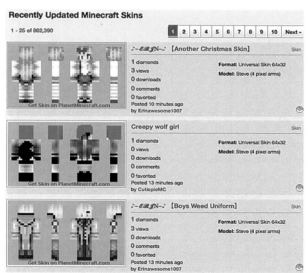

Top: The page on minecraft.net where skins can be changed for PC/Mac/Linux. Middle: A few minutes on any big Minecraft server will show you the wild variety of skins that are out there. Bottom: A typical selection of fan-made skins on PlanetMinecraft.

button at the top of the screen. Sign into your profile, and the very next page will ask you if you want to change your skin. All you do then is to select one of the two character models (the only difference is that one has slightly skinnier arms), and then you click "Browse" and find the skin file on your computer. After that it's just a matter of uploading the file! Super simple, all around.

**Console:** Skins on console versions are changed in the game menu when you're in a game. Skins are located under the Help & Options menu, and though you can't upload custom or self-made skins like you can for PC or Mac, there are many, many skinpacks available on console to purchase, most of which have a free trial with a few free skins in them.

**Where to Get Skins**
Kind of a creepy sentence, no? Well, in this case, we're talkin' the non-fleshy kind of skins, so don't worry. Skins for the PC and Mac version are readily available online in the thousands, and finding them is as simple as heading to a skin database (another creepy phrase!) and just picking one out and downloading it.

A few of the biggest skin databases include Planet Minecraft, The Skindex, MinecraftSkins.net and the SkinCache.

**Making Your Own Skin**
The creepy sentences keep coming! Making your own skin is a pretty simple process, as all skins are actually just a flat image that is wrapped around the character model. A wide variety of programs exists out there to help you create and test skins yourself, and it does not take much time to become a master skinner. Some of the best include NovaSkin, Miners Need Cool Shoes and MCSkinner, the first two of which are actually used completely online in a browser. The Minecraft Wiki has a great list of skinning programs to check out if creating your own look interests you, so just Google "Minecraft skin program," and you'll see the list.

# Resource/Texture Packs

Where skins change the look of your character, resource packs, also called texture packs, change the look of the actual blocks in your game. They can also change things like the way Water looks and the way the sky and even the sun and moon appear, making them very powerful tools to create a new experience in your game.

**How to Change**

PC/Mac- Mojang has included a nice little shortcut in Minecraft to make adding a new resource pack quite easy. Simply start up the game, and then go to Options in the menus. Click on Resource Packs, and then hit the Open Resource Pack Folder button. You'll then need to either quit the game or turn Fullscreen to OFF in the Video settings, and you will see a window open that is the folder named Resource Packs. Then, simply copy-paste the .zip resource pack files that you want to add into the folder!

Top: Changing resource packs is simply a matter of navigating to the right menu after you instal them. Middle: Even the menus can look quite different when you load up a resource pack. Bottom: Minecraft almost looks like a totally new game with packs, so experiment and find one that makes your world look the best!

**Console:** Like skins, resource packs on the console are limited to the ones that are officially available, but there are quite a few of these out there. On the console, resource packs are officially known as "texture packs," and they must be loaded before you load the actual game world. It's actually one of the options when you select a world, right there on the screen as you confirm your selection, and you simply pick the one you want. Like skins, you can also purchase extra texture packs if you wish for pretty cheap ($1).

## Where to Get Resource/Texture Packs

Resource/texture packs for the PC and Mac can also be found online, again at sites like Planet Minecraft, resourcepack.net, MinecraftTexturePacks.net and Curse's Minecraft Texture Packs page. The Minecraft Forum is perhaps the best place to get packs, as you'll see players upload them and update very frequently, and it provides a great place for other players to post pictures of their worlds with the packs turned on and discuss them.

## Making Your Own Resource Packs

This is also totally possible, though it is much, much more intensive than creating a Minecraft skin. Again, there are a wide variety of programs out there to help you out with this, and using Google to find the Minecraft Wiki's Resource Pack Creators page is your best bet. Successfully creating a resource pack is a pretty big undertaking however, as you'll need to think carefully about how every texture you create will look in your world and together with the textures of other blocks. We'd suggest using YouTube to get some tutorials on the specific program you choose, which should help tremendously.

The same scene in a variety of shaders. Particularly note the differences in the Water, the shadows and the way the focus works.

# Shaders

Shaders are by far the most powerful visuals-changing feature of the game, as they actually change the way that light and pixels are displayed. When you've seen those really gorgeous photos of Minecraft with lots of realistic shadows and lighting effects, they are always created in a Minecraft world that has shaders enabled. It's by far one of the most dramatic ways to change your game, with some players saying that they simply can't go back to playing without shaders on. However, shaders are PC/Mac/Linux only, they're somewhat difficult to install, and they require a pretty powerful computer to be able to run and actually play the game (and not just take a quick screenshot).

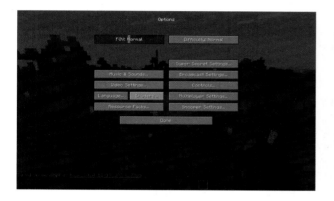 

### How to Change

There are a few built-in shaders for Minecraft on the computer, which can be found by clicking the "Super Secret Settings" button in the menus in-game. However, these are mostly just pixel shaders and not very good to play with. The shaders that people use to actually play the game require that you install the Forge modloader (files and instructions at files.minecraftforge.net), and you then need to install the Shaders Mod (found at http://bit.ly/ShadersModLink with instructions).

Once this is installed, you'll need to make a shaderpacks folder in your main Minecraft folder (the same place where you find the folders for your screenshots, saves and mods), and then download and place shaderpacks into the shaderpacks folder. Once you've got it all set up

like the instructions at the Shaders Mod page tell you, you'll be able to load your Forge mod profile through the Minecraft launcher, open a world, and then hit the ESC key to go to your options. In your Video settings you will now have a Shaders option, where you can select which shader you want to use.

### Where to Get Shaders

There aren't nearly as many shaders out there to download as skins and resource packs, but some of our favorites, and the ones used in this book, include Sonic Ether's Unbelievable Shaders, Sildur's Vibrant Shaders, MrMeep_x3's Shaders and DocteurDread's Shaders. Most of these have their own page on the Forums, so just Google the name and you'll find them easily.

# Mini-Games Galore!

Ah, mini-games! Those saviors of Minecraft that take our vanilla-jaded minds and turn them onto something new and awesome that makes Minecraft feel like a whole new game.

Of course, we do love vanilla Minecraft, but after countless dozens of hours, even the world's best game can get a little old hat. Lucky for us Crafters, Minecraft is set up so that it is ideal for intrepid creators around the world to modify and turn into all sorts of other games.

Servers like mc.hypixel.net are where mini-games not only get played, but created and tested by thousands upon thousands of players each day.

We call these mini-games, and they're essentially just alternative ways to play Minecraft. Some of them are just slight tweaks to the Survival Mode that manage to make it feel entirely new and unique, while others barely resemble anything you'd see or do in a regular game of vanilla Crafting.

As we've done with the last few editions of our book, here are a few of our favorite current mini-games in the Minecraft world today, as well as a bit more info on some of the modes we've talked about in the past.

# Factions

**Type: Long-Term Complex Survival Variant**

Factions is among the most popular Minecraft mini-games, and it's also one of the most in-depth when it comes to what you can do. The basic idea is that you are in a regular Survival world with many other players (typically there's no limit to the amount), but you have the added ability to join a faction.

Factions are essentially teams of players that can claim a "chunk" of land for their faction. Only players that are members of the faction can open chests or build or destroy anything by hand on a faction's land. Non-members will find themselves unable to affect another faction's land, except by using TNT, Lava or Water dropped onto it. Typically, you can't be hurt on your faction's claimed land as well.

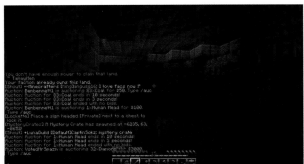

Factions has a very active chat with auctions and a multitude of chat commands that are important to your game.

Playing Factions is best done with friends, whether those you know in the real world or those met online, because a one person faction can't get much done. Find a faction to join, or get some buddies together to make one of your own!

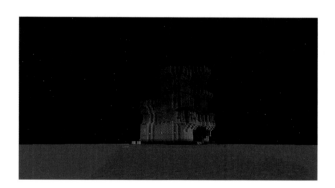

Land chunks extend from the bedrock to sky and can be claimed by using Power, which each player has in a certain amount, and some of which is lost when the player dies. Usually a player starts with 10 Power, claims land using 1 Power and loses 3 Power on death, but this can be different between servers. When a player joins a faction, their Power is added to the faction total, allowing the faction to claim more land. Be warned though: when you lose Power from dying, that Power will be subtracted from your faction's total. If your faction ever has less power than it has claimed chunks of land, you can start to lose that land. Over time, your Power can grow back, thankfully, but this happens very, very slowly.

The goal of Factions is to grow your faction, get more money (used to buy items and/or land), recruit new faction members and declare war against or ally up with other factions. So basically, it turns (almost) vanilla Minecraft into an all out tribal war. It's a never-ending brutal war for domination and land, and it's one heck of a cool way to compete in Minecraft over an extended period of time.

Top and Middle: Flying Snowballs are a common sight in Paintball; in fact you'll probably never see so many in the air at once anywhere else in Minecraft! Bottom: Each match of Paintball has players select a team by picking a colored Wool block in a little pre-game room.

# Paintball

**Type:** One-Shot-Kill Deathmatch

If Factions seem a little too much commitment and effort for your Minecrafting session, Paintball is on the opposite side of the spectrum of mini-games in that it's quick, easy and doesn't require much knowledge of the ins and outs of Minecraft.

Paintball is pretty easy to pick up: all you do is run around a map trying to hit players with "paintballs," which are actually just Snowballs under a different name. If you hit a player once, they are immediately warped back to spawn and you and your team get points. The first team to get a certain amount of points or the team with the most points after a set amount of time wins. On some servers getting "kills" earns you coins that you can use to purchase powerups for either you or your team, like a triple-shot or reducing the amount of deaths your team has.

And that's it! Pretty simple, no? Don't be fooled though; while picking up a game of Paintball is easy and you're probably going to get at least a few kills in every match you play, there are some players that have taken this little mini-game rather seriously indeed and can hit other players with ease from far across the map. With practice, though, you can become one of these skillshot aficionados and start to get your name in the Top 3 of the scoresheet with regularity.

# TNT Run

**Type:** No Weapon Spleef Variant

A game that seems easy, and is another simple one to understand, but which will put your jumping and navigational skills to the test like few others. TNT Run has been around for a long time, and it involves running around in an arena on a flat surface which will fall out underneath you as you go. That means that if you step on a block, you better move quick because soon that block will drop and you'll fall to the next layer below.

The idea is to keep moving around and create holes in the ground as you move that other players fall into. Since these players are creating more holes themselves, you'll need to keep on your toes and plan out where you run, deftly jumping any holes that you can't run around.

When you fall to the next layer, you'll do the same thing there, and the player that is able to keep from falling through the final layer of the arena and into the darkness below is the winner.

Some players get a little confused about TNT Run's name, as there are no explosions in this mini-game. The reason the game is named after the 'splodiest block in Minecraft is that there is a block of TNT under each block that makes up the layers of the arena. The game has been specially designed so that walking on the Sand or Gravel blocks that make up the floor of each layer causes the TNT to activate beneath the Sand or Gravel, causing the Sand or Gravel to fall, though without causing an explosion. Essentially it's just a trick to get the game to work, so no need to worry about getting blown up in this mini-game. Just worry about where you're going to put your feet next!

Top and Middle: As you can see from these images, the maps in Wizards get absolutely wrecked by the end of a match, which is a major part of the fun. Bottom: Select your Wizard class before each match, or you can let it assign you one automatically.

# Wizards

**Type:** Magic Kit Command Point PVP

Who doesn't want to be a wizard? We know we're into the idea of wrathfully slingin' the powers of magic at our foes, and that's why we love the Wizards mini-game. This one is a simple PVP "capture the command point" mode that has each player pick a team and a kit, and each kit is a different type of wizard with a variety of unique powers.

The powers and wizard-types run the gamut from fireball throwers to ice wizards and more, and each class typically has an exploding spell attack that has a special feature to it, like a fireball that burns enemies (a Fire Charge shot when a staff is used), and a special defensive power, like an instant teleport. Most powers take "mana," which in this case is the icons in your hunger bar, which are used up quickly but also regenerate very quickly. Once you've selected your wizard-type, it's locked in for the rest of the match, so make sure to try a few out and find one you're good with.

The red pad with the beam of light coming out of it is one of the command points in a Wizards match, which you need to go stand on in order to secure it for your team.

## Here's the list of Wizards classes and their powers:

### FIRE WIZARD
**Attack Power:** Launches a fireball
**Defense Power:** Instant teleportation

### KINETIC WIZARD
**Attack Power:** High damage, short-range railgun
**Defense Power:** Gravity gun

### ICE WIZARD
**Attack Power:** Freeze shot to slow enemies
**Defense Power:** Puts up a wall of Ice

### WITHER WIZARD
**Attack Power:** Exploding extra-poisonous Wither skull shot
**Defense Power:** An extra row of "absorption hearts"

### BLOOD WIZARD
**Attack Power:** Normal attack costs 2 hearts instead of mana
**Defense Power:** Has a Splash Potion that instantly regenerates health

The matches themselves are set in an arena that is decently sized and typically contains all destructible blocks, which makes Wizards somewhat unique to PVP matches, which often feature indestructible arenas. Wizards arenas are like this because the powers at the disposal of each wizard in the match are mighty forces of nature that tend to explode and cause area damage, and part of the fun of Wizards matches is that the explosions wreck the environment as the match goes along. And, since the gravity is much lower in Wizards matches, you can jump just about anywhere, making every block in the arena part of the battleground. By the time a winner is announced, the whole arena will be in glorious ruins.

The combat in Wizards is a little different from many such fast-paced PVP mini-games; although your spells have spectacular effects and do damage in an area, each wizard is actually pretty tough to kill and will not go down without more than a couple direct hits. Additionally, you aren't just trying to kill your enemies, you're also trying to walk on two different command points so that you capture them for your team. If enemy players are on the command point, they will start capturing it for their team instead, and the more players from one team on the command point, the more likely it is to go to that team. Once it's been captured, the other team has to keep enemy players off it to capture it back, otherwise it will keep going fully back to the team that last captured it.

Points rack up for a team based on the amount of time a command point has been owned by that team, and when one team reaches 2,000 points, they win this mighty struggle of magic users.

Wizards is as chaotic as it gets, but its balance of excellent unique classes, destructible terrain, low gravity, heavily armored players and the PVP + command points structure makes for one of the best PVP experiences in the world of Minecraft.

After the initial countdown, players rush from their starting points to the Chests in the center (middle image), after which it's an all-out fight for survival across a decently large map, though one that's smaller and faster than that of most Survival Games matches.

# Blitz

**Type:** Fast Survival Games Variant

Survival Games is one of the most popular mini-games, and it has been for a long time, but Blitz is our favorite version of Survival Games. It takes the basic concept of an arena with Chests with items scattered around it and kit selection and makes the competition much fiercer and quicker by having smaller arenas, crazier kits and a special Blitz Star that spawns every so often and gives the finder extra powers.

There are a *ton* of kits in Blitz (far too many to list here), each of which has very specific traits and powers, and each of which can be upgraded from level I to level X. Some of the kits are free, while others require winning and purchasing to access, and the level of the kit determines the amount and quality of items you get from it and your appearance.

Games of Blitz start out like other Survival Games matches, with players spread out evenly in a circle around a group of Chests. When the countdown finishes, players are able to move and can either risk running to the Chests to try and get items before other players, or they can just run off into the map. PVP is immediately enabled in Blitz, but the items from your kit will not appear in your inventory until 60 seconds into the match. The arenas are decently sized with

many hiding spots, and they also contain quite a few hidden Chests, which contain random items like those in the center of the spawn point.

Strategy in Blitz is fairly complex and requires quick changes and thinking. You'll have to decide whether to risk going for Chests or simply to hide and wait for your kit, and you'll be playing against all sorts of other kits, including those that are far above your level. Being higher level does not necessarily guarantee a kill in Blitz, however, as it is still pretty easy to kill someone with a good kit if you catch them at the right time with the right items, especially before they get their kit. You also have a player tracker in the form of a compass, which will show you the direction of the closest player, which can help both offensively and defensively. Because of these reasons, good kits are highly useful, but not a game-breaker.

The Blitz Star, while also not a breaker, certainly is a game changer, as it spawns randomly on the map every 5 minutes and allows the finder to select from a variety of special one-time boosts. There are 18 of these, and they can do everything

from teleporting to the closest player and dealing 10 damage, making all arrows one-shot-kill players for a 30 second period, steal hit points from players in a radius around the player, give extra regeneration and much more. All Blitz Stars also give Regeneration II for 30 seconds, which is useful all on its own.

Combine all of this together, and you get a very complex game that moves much quicker than regular Survival Games, which can sometimes go on for a very long time. Typically many players are killed before they even get their kits in the first 60 seconds of each match, but that being said, the last few players in a game of Blitz can often still take a decent amount of time to pick each other off.

While Survival Games is still going strong as one of the top mini-games for Minecraft, we think Blitz gives it a little kick-in-the-pants both in terms of pacing and complexity (with the addition of the Blitz Star and better kits) that makes us favor it over the original. Of course, that's not too surprising considering that this mini-game is one of the always-great Hypixel server creations.

# A Guide To Winning Ultra Hardcore:
## Minecraft's Best Mini Game

If horse racing is the sport of kings, Ultra HardCore or UHC is the mini-game of Minecraft monarchs. By that we mean it's the game for the very best of the best when it comes to Minecraft, and only those players who truly know what they're doing in survival mode can ever hope to last for more than 20 minutes or so, much less win a game of UHC. Go peep the YouTube

## NOTE:

Hiding your achievements is an excellent UHC strategy, because knowing what another player is doing is extremely helpful to defeating them in this mode. You can do this by having just one player on a team craft all of your Crafting Tables, handing them out to the other players. You get the "Benchmarking" achievement only when you pick up a Crafting Table from the output slot of either your inventory crafting menu or from a Crafting Table output. Since you have to get achievements in a specific order in order to get the next one, skipping the Benchmarking achievement will mean that your achievements stop showing, even if you complete the necessary action. This will help spread confusion and disinformation, giving you a distinct advantage. Does not work in single player UHC, however, unless you steal someone else's Crafting Table.

channels of any member of the Mindcrack Network, which regularly engages in riveting UHC brawls, to see the kind of skills it takes to get good at this mini-game.

What makes UHC so gosh darned hard? Well, that'd be in the name: it's not just Hardcore Mode, which means one death and you're out, it's Ultra HardCore mode, which means it's hard to impossible to even heal. Otherwise it's a fight to the death in Survival Mode, typically on a small (and sometimes shrinking!) map, but the fact that you have to be very careful not to even lose one heart carelessly is what makes UHC so hard, and so thrilling.

While learning to be the best of the best at UHC requires mastery of just about all things Survival, meaning you'll want to simply learn all you can about the game, this is a mini-guide to the mode that will give you a leg up on your opponents and make you much more likely to survive. Remember though: these are just tips! UHC is all about general Minecraft knowledge and adaptability, so make sure to learn about the basics of the game as well, and never be afraid to try a bold new strategy if it makes sense in the situation.

**1. Don't waste time, especially at the beginning.** You simply can't mess around when playing UHC, especially right at the beginning. While later stages of the match are harder to do with perfect efficiency, like Diamond/Gold hunting or Arrow creating, everything you need to do at the beginning can be

done either right or wrong. That is to say, you can be quick about it, or you can do it badly. When you start a match of UHC, you need to acquire food, Wood, Crafting Tables and basic gear as quickly as you can, or else another team or competitor will be ahead of you and thus much more likely to win.

**2. Know the specific rules of the server and the match.** Not all UHC matches are the same. Some spawn you with a gear kit, some have shrinking borders, some allow healing with potions while others only allow it with Golden Apples or not at all. Know the rules of the specific server you're on and the match you're in, or else you may spend a lot of time trying to do something that just won't work.

**3. Be entirely overly careful.** Do not take damage from anything except a player or a mob, and avoid that at all costs. Falling damage or damage from Lava, drowning or hitting a teammate is really something that should not happen in a UHC match, and if it does, it means you are less likely to win. Paranoia based security is the name of the game: if it seems even a little dangerous, get away from it ASAP. Do not make risky jumps if possible, stay out of dark places when possible (even dark forests) and run away from all hostile mobs (especially Skeletons), don't even get near Lava in most situations. It's just not worth it unless you have awesome armor, which you won't for a while.

**4. Get the right resources, ignore the others.** Not everything is useful in UHC. Here's a list of things you want, everything else can be ignored or dropped for the most part:

• **Raw resources:** Wood, Coal, Iron, Gold, Diamond, Emerald (Emerald only in case you see a Village— Lapis Lazuli (for enchanting in v1.8 or above)

• **Food, especially Apples but do not eat Apples** (they are for making Golden Apples)

• **Feathers and Flint** (for Arrows)

• **Sugar Cane and Leather** (to make Books for enchanting)

• **Obsidian** (for Enchanting Table, best made instead of hunted)

• **String** (for Bows)

**Specialty items for specific strategies:**
• **Bones** (to tame Wolves who will fight for you)

• **Brewing items** (Sand/Glass, Blaze Rods and Nether Wart etc., to make Potions. Very, very dangerous but can work if done carefully.)

**5. Go underground quickly.** Once you've gathered whatever food you can on the surface and have plenty of Wood, Crafting Tables and basic tools, you need to get underground and start hunting ores and Spiders ASAP. The best option is to find caves and follow them, or safely go down a ravine, but if you can't find any of these quickly, go ahead and just start digging down in a staircase. You need ore, because as our next step says…

**6. Gear is essential.** Gear is what will make you win or lose UHC. Outside of ambushes and accidents, the people with the best gear almost always win the match, so it is your number one priority. Gear is important in the following order, with the most important at the the top, and you would do well to focus on acquiring each in this order:

* Stone Sword and tools
* Armor (the best kind you can make)
* Food
* Better Sword, and Bow and Arrows (equally important)
* Golden Apples
* Potions

**7. Consider the Nether.** This is very risky, but there are also massive benefits if you survive. The Nether will put you away from most other players, who will be scared to venture there, and it will give you the opportunity to collect Blaze Rods and Nether Wart to make potions. However, do not go to the Nether if you are not very, very good at surviving in it, and never go without at least Iron Armor, a Bow and an Iron Sword, if not better gear.

**8. Be sneaky and vigilant at all times.** Many players in UHC get killed simply because they were focusing too much on resource hunting and gear crafting and they didn't notice that someone was sneaking up on them. Make sure you're scanning your surroundings for other players at all times, and try to stay out of sight or underground whenever possible. Also, use the darkness trick to see other players' nametags: dig a hole or place blocks on all sides of you so that you are in total darkness, then look in every direction. If there is any player near you, you'll see their nametag. Beware though: other players use this trick, so if you think someone might be looking for you, go into sneak mode with the crouch key. This hides your nametag, allowing you to remain safely hidden.

**9. Pay attention to coordinates.** It's a good idea to keep your coordinates up and watch them at all times. This is because you want to know where you've been in order not to go over the same area repeatedly, and so you know where you are in relation to the center of the map. The center is where players will most often have to pass through, making it the most dangerous area as well as the best hunting grounds. This strategy is especially important for matches with shrinking maps.

**10. Bring the fight to the enemy.** When you're all geared up, don't just wait around for other players to ambush them. Do this some, but do it on the move. A player that's moving is much harder to target and is much more likely to get the drop on other players and defeat them. If you're geared up, be bold and take the fight to your enemies, but of course do this stealthily and carefully.

There is little in Minecraft as rewarding as outsmarting, out-surviving and simply outcrafting everyone else in a UHC match. It's thrilling, nail-biting fun that we can't recommend enough, and with this little guide, you are much more likely to come out on top.

---

**NOTE:** This is not as common a game on servers as some of the other mini-games, primarily because it's challenging, but also because it takes a bit of time and quite a few people to play. A match can last anywhere from 30 minutes to three or four hours, and it's best played with at least 8 people or 4 teams. That being said, it's the pinnacle of Minecraft competition, and it should be played by all Crafters.

# Spotlight Corner: Servers And Mods

Nothing gives Minecraft more life, extended playability and new thrills like the servers and mods that users have built around this game. What started as a simple mining game has gone places Notch likely never dreamed of through the work of the intrepid creators on the modding and server designing fronts. In fact, when most players first discover either of these communities, they tend to feel like they're playing an entirely different game, though the blocky graphics tell them that it's still Minecraft.

It might look like Minecraft, but these servers and mods take Minecraft's unbeatable adaptability and turn the game into just about anything that creators can think of. Want to play an MMO version of Minecraft, complete with skill trees, classes, a giant world and quests? That's out there. Feel like a silly Smash Bros. style brawl of quickness and chaos? Definitely exists. Want to turn into a hamster, fly to the moon and create a colony of Pokemon? Those are all mods, and there are servers that host each and every one of them.

This is our list of the mods and servers we think are absolutely killing it right now, and if you or anyone you know have ever expressed boredom with vanilla Minecraft, we'd bet that just a single one of these will get you right back into the blocky fray. These are just a handful of the many, many servers and mods that exist as well, so if you like anything here, chances are there are at least a dozen more out there that you'll dig just as much .

So without further ado, here's our newest edition of the hot mods and servers list to get your little Diamond-loving selves into.

# Servers: Worlds Waiting for You Online

As varied as one person's Minecraft world is from another, servers are even crazier. There are plain Survival and Creative servers, role playing servers, competition servers, Factions servers and infinite more variations, and servers can hold as few as 0 other people or as many as 10,000+! It's one of the best parts of Minecraft, and each of the servers in our list here is absolutely worth at least a little peeking around.

## 2b2t

**Server Address: 2b2t.org**

So…2b2t is crazy. It is a world where the idea is that anything goes, at all, and it is not supposed to be reset ever. Unfortunately, it was reset once recently, due to the need for an update, but this is actually kind of good because as 2b2t goes along, it gets outright wild. This server is really like no other, and in fact, it's like no other thing in gaming. Because people cheat wildly, grief relentlessly and absolutely wreck the area for thousands of blocks around the spawn, 2b2t's landscape turns into a nightmare wasteland which you will probably not survive. Be warned: 2b2t is not for the faint of heart or the sensitive. You will die, people will attack you and wreck/steal whatever you have, and you will very likely run into some offensive language and behavior here. That being said, it's an experience like no other and completely fun, if you're ready for what awaits you.

# Arkham Network

**Server Address: mc.arkhamnetwork.org**

The Arkham Network consistently comes up in best-of lists for Minecraft servers because it is one of the most well-oiled and fun competitive servers that exist today. You'll almost always find thousands of other players on the Arkham Network no matter when you log in, and it features a semi-rotating crop of the most popular styles of play and mini-games, adding more as they are invented. As Minecraft communities go, this is one of the strongest, and they take entertaining you with mini-games very seriously.

One of the best parts of big servers like Arkham network is that everything from the hub to the mini-game maps is professionally designed and looks amazing.

Typically images like these would come from Creative servers, but Empire is a special place! Their unique rules and world structure allows for awesome town plots like these in a Survival Mode server.

# Empire

**Server Address: play.emc.gs**

It may surprise some of you to learn that the server in these images, Empire Minecraft, is actually a Survival server. Yes, it looks like a Creative Mode server, but that's because Empire employs a very interesting system wherein players live in a Survival world, but are given plots of protected land within a giant town on the server. So, though players can die and explore the world like a normal survival server outside of town, they end up building enormous, oft-amazing creations within the huge city that has built up in Empire. Additionally, there are other add-ons to vanilla Minecraft to be found here, including new mobs and bosses and an economy system.

# Extronus

**Server Address: pvp.extronus.net**

Extronus' Factions zones are very nicely designed with interesting aesthetics like this ice world look, as opposed to the typical vanilla world that many Factions servers contain.

Most servers choose either vanilla Minecraft, Creative Mode or do many mini-games, but not Extronus. No, here the players are about one thing and one thing only: Factions. A part of the Arkham Network that has grown into its own thing, Extronus takes this mini-game to the extreme by creating an entire, thriving server dedicated to it, and the culture there is pretty intensely into the game. There are actually a few Factions servers rolled into one server hub here, each of which has an awesome aesthetic theme that has been handcrafted, such as the ice world you see in the photo. As they say in Extronus "Choose YOUR path and build your Empire."

# Hypixel

**Server Address: mc.hypixel.net**

Few servers can boast either hubs as gorgeous as Hypixel's or mini-games as fun and creative.

The great Hypixel's personally hosted server, hypixel.net is another quality competition/PvP server and one of the more frequented servers online. Since it is run by one of the bigger personalities in the game, you'll often find "celeb" players here as well as a very well-updated list of mini-games and competitions. Plus, because of the quality of folks involved, everything in it runs very smoothly and looks incredible! In fact, many mini-games were actually created specifically for this server, like the Blitz game we profile in our Mini-Games chapter of this book. Hypixel's home is a benchmark server for other servers, in that it's where trends are born and server methods are perfected, so why not spend a little time at one of the web's best locations?

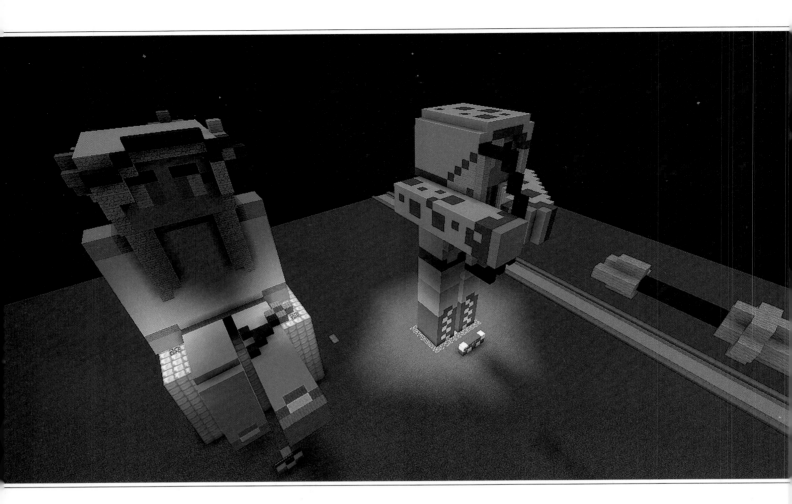

# Lichcraft

**Server Address: us.lichcraft.com**

Consistently ranked among the top (if not at the top) servers online, Lichcraft is similar to Hypixel and the Arkham Network but with a few different games to play, including Survival, Skygrid, kit PVP, Duels, Prison, MineZ and an excellent couple of Factions servers that are well populated and nicely run. It's just a solid server all around, and that's why it continues to be one of the best-known and most frequented servers in the game.

A personal favorite of this author, Lichcraft is a server that has just about every major mode and does all of it well.

# MindCrack

**Server Address: us.playmindcrack.com**

There are actually two MindCrack servers (at least): the private one played on by Guude and the other members of the famous MindCrack Network, which is the subject of many incredibly popular YouTube video series, and then the public MindCrack server, which is this one. While it's pretty hard to get an invitation to the private MindCrack server, the public server is an example of the highest quality server that a regular Minecrafter can get on. Not only can you tour the maps from old seasons of the MindCrack video series, literally stepping virtual foot where some of the best Crafters in the world once built, you can also play the mini-games created by this untouchably talented crew of builders and YouTubers. Many of the great Redstone engineer SethBling's mini-game creations are tested first on this server, such as the wild and explosive Missile Wars game he created with Cubehamster, and indeed most of the mini-games found here are not seen elsewhere. Along with 2b2t, Hypixel and WesterosCraft, the MindCrack server sits among online royalty when it comes to public servers.

Here you see the team select for the awesome Mineplex Arcade, and the image above is of one of the games featured in said Arcade. In this game every player looks like a Villager and is in a sea of real Villagers. You have to try and figure out who is real and kill them, and every so often everyone changes into their normal form for a few seconds. Super fun!

# Mineplex

**Server Address: us.mineplex.com**

A top mini-game server, Mineplex typically is one of the very busiest servers, often with over 10,000 players online at a time. In fact, at the time of this writing it has a whopping 13,354 Minecrafters on it enjoying the entertainment it has to offer. Mineplex is professionally run, with server hosts that really pay attention to the desires of their virtual denizens and who are constantly adding new features, tweaking things to be better and throwing special events just to make things that much more fun. Maybe one of the best features on any server is Mineplex's Arcade where they mix up a ton of fun mini-games that play one after the other, so you only have to load into a lobby once.

Treasure Island takes Creative Mode quite seriously, as is readily apparent when you spend a little time around the 0,0 coordinates, where most of the oldest and best plots are located.

# Treasure Island

**Server Address: ticreative.org**

Treasure Island is actually a collection of servers, like many of the others on this list, and it hosts many of the popular styles from PvP to Skyblock, but for here we're focusing on the subserver that focuses on Creative Mode. This is because the Treasure Island Creative server is incredible when it comes to the amount and quality of builds that can be found there. In fact, Treasure Island goes so far as to have a whole series of islands to build on and a system where players can judge other players' creations and give them points that earn ranks. The higher rank you are, the more islands you have access to build on, meaning that some islands are exclusively built on by those players that the community deems to be most skilled.

# WesterosCraft

**Server Address: mc.westeroscraft.com , but has its own special launcher that should be used**

Now, there are probably other servers out there with builders as skilled and dedicated as those at WesterosCraft, but frankly, we've never seen one that beats it. If you want an example of what a truly talented and committed group of people can do with their time, this is the server that you want to check out. The idea is that they are building a detail-oriented replica of the world from the A Song of Ice and Fire books and the Game of Thrones TV show, including both the giant continent of Westeros and the bigger continent of Essos. This project has been going along for years, and they've built an area that is, as they say, about the size of Los Angeles in real life. While the locations they've painstakingly crafted are all stunning, perhaps even more impressive are the incredible server testing grounds located around the 3D map of the world, where the master builders that put this server together try out their creations before doing them for real. If you want to learn how to be a better builder in any way, from the creation of buildings all the way down to trees (they have a whole forest of tester trees, each in its own labeled square, and it's quite beautiful), you could not do better than to spend some time just flying over the WesterosCraft testing grounds. Good people of WesterosCraft, the writers of this book salute your efforts as truly awesome in the original sense of the word.

# Mods: Change Up the Game

We've always said that what you can do in Minecraft is limited only by your imagination, and while it's true that you can build just about anything you can think of in the regular game, there's another facet of Minecraft that takes the game and truly does turn it into whatever the human mind can come up with. They're called mods, short for modifications, and they are little bits of code written by fans just like yourself that add amazing new features or change Minecraft in unbelievable and super cool ways. These are some of the best ones out there, and they run the gamut from the small and quirky to the mods that change literally everything about the game of Minecraft.

## Tekkit

**Installed through:** Technic Launcher
**Minecraft Version Compatible:** Automatic
**Link:** bit.ly/TechnicTekkit

Tekkit is one of the big boys of the modding scene, having been around for quite some time and being not just one mod, but a whole pack of them. If you're new to modding, this is the one we'd suggest you go with first, as it's both chock full of some of the best mod content around and it's super easy to use. What's nice about Technic's packs is that you only have to get their launcher to run them; you don't have to worry about version compatibility or moving files around at all. Plus, the production value is just amazing on their launcher. In terms of what Tekkit contains, it has about two dozen mods all packed together, with the idea that you are adding an immense amount of building items and technology (hence "Tekkit") like factory mechanisms, rocketships and powersuits to your Minecraft. A much loved, highly recommended mod experience.

# Mine and Blade

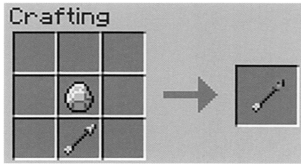

Like many mods, Mine and Blade adds quite a lot of new craftable items, like this expensive Diamond Arrow.

**Installed through:** Forge (manually place .jar file in mods folder)

**Minecraft Version Compatible:** 1.7.10

**Link:** bit.ly/MineandBlade

Actually called Mine and Blade Battlegear 2 for this version, this is a Modpack that is named after the war simulation battle game Mount & Blade and which adds a very large amount of things to kill other Crafters and mobs with to your game. That is to say, it's chock full of weapons! While many Modpacks add weapons, Mine and Blade is considered one of the best, and it even adds the ability to use a shield and dual-wield some killing implements.

This odd machine bores tunnels into whatever is in front of it, allowing you to save a little bit of time and hard work.

# Railcraft

**Installed through:** Forge (manually place .jar file in mods folder)

**Minecraft Version Compatible:** 1.7.10

**Link:** bit.ly/RailCraftMod

The Rails system in Minecraft is actually pretty primitive when compared to even the most basic real-world train track, and the popular Railcraft mod sets that wrong right, and then some. It adds all manner of new tracks and cart items, as well as fixing some pesky issues with Minecarts, such as making the physics more realistic. It sounds simple, but the things you can do with Railcraft get quite complex and can lead to some really amazing automated builds, as well doing some fun things like giving you a new way to dig cool looking tunnels for trains and giving you a "Launch Track," which does just what it sounds like it would.

# Mutant Creatures

**Installed through:** Forge (manually place .jar file in mods folder)
**Minecraft Version Compatible:** 1.7.10
**Link:** bit.ly/MutantCreaturesMCMod

An example of a couple of the awesome mutated mobs you'll get from this little mod (top image by Anikaitgarg, bottom by Ben101994).

Ever looked at an Enderman and thought, "Enderman, you just aren't weird enough!" With the Mutant Creatures mod, it's unlikely you'll be doing that ever again, as its whole premise is to take the plain versions of mobs and seriously weird them up. Mobs get bigger, really freaky lookin', and have much more strength and better attacks. In a fun twist, this mod also allows you to create minion Creepers, which will attempt to aid you against the mutants' onslaught by blowin' 'em right up. Watch out though- they might get overexcited and accidentally catch you in the explosion too!

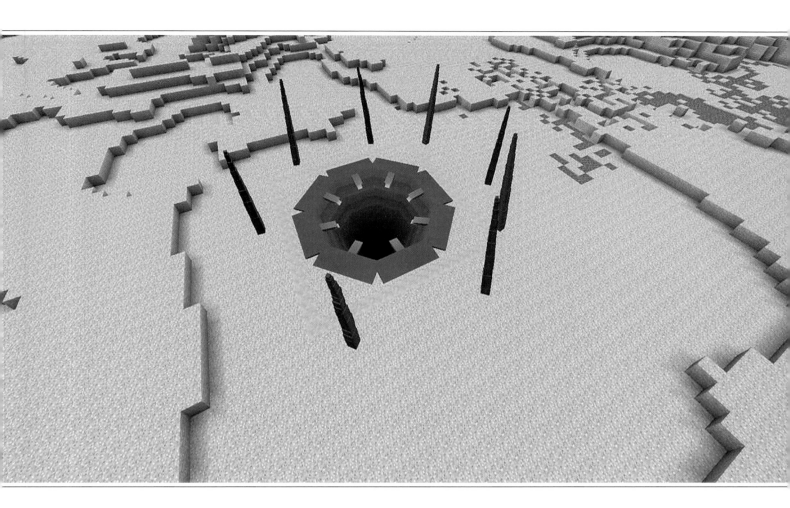

This mod inserts all manner of *Star Wars* items and creatures into Minecraft, like the dreaded Sarlacc above and this electrostaff below.

# Minecraft Star Wars Mod

**Installed through:** Forge (manually place .jar file in mods folder)

**Minecraft Version Compatible:** 1.7.2

**Link:** bit.ly/StarWarsMCMod

*Star Wars* makes everything better, and Minecraft is no exception. Those who have dreamed of using a lightsaber or hanging out with R2-D2 in Minecraft need dream no longer, and those who never have might want to try and get some cooler dreams. This mod is a nerd's fantasy come true, and it'll have you feeling like you're crossing the sands of Tatooine on the way to Tosche Station for some power converters in no time flat.

It ain't hard to see why A Era do Futuro is so popular. Even the trees are different and amazing, as seen in this shot of the included Twilight Forest mod by wikispaces!

# A Era do Futuro

**Installed through:** Technic Launcher
**Minecraft Version Compatible:** Automatic
**Link:** bit.ly/AEraDo

Of the Technic modpacks, A Era do Futuro is the most popular, and for good reason: it contains over 40 of the Minecraft world's most beloved mods. In a nutshell, it overhauls pretty much every facet of the game, including the biomes (with mod Extra Biomes XL), the mobs (Mo'Zombies, Mutant Creatures, Primitive Mobs and more), the weapons (Asgard Shield, Legend Gear, More Bows and more) and just about everything else. With A Era do Futuro, you'll be able to build amazing machines, fly to space, travel through a fantasy forest dimension and ever so much more, making it one of the best modpacks to wet your whistle with when starting out.

A typical idyllic floating island scene from an Aether world by gilded games. Don't fall off, now!

# The Aether

**Installed through:** Instructions at link page
**Minecraft Version Compatible:** 1.7.3
**Link:** bit.ly/TheAetherForum

The Aether mod adds a new dimension to your world that is the polar opposite of the Nether. The Aether is a sky dimension, and it keeps with that theme by including flying animals (Pigs with wings!), lots of cloud-based items and a very fluffy and light look and feel. It's also a huge challenge however, as it adds in three neat little Aether dungeons that have dangerous mobs and bosses in them, and each of which has a reward.

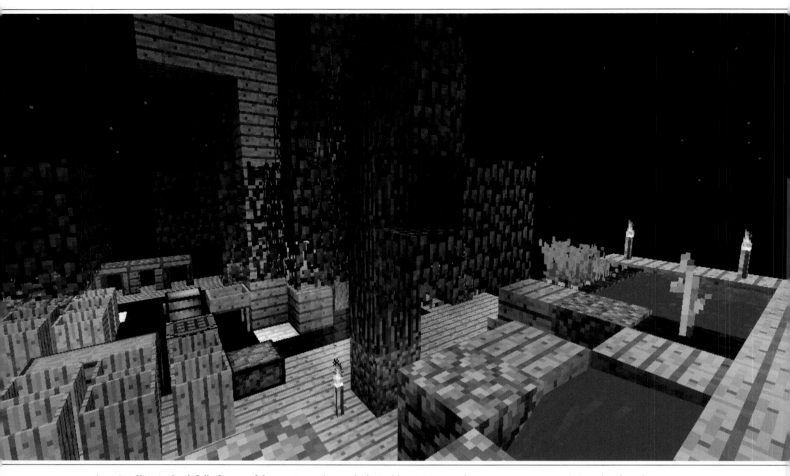

Agrarian Skies is chock full of some of the most popular mods that add new items and systems to your game. In just this shot alone you see Barrels, a new type of Chest, a Half-Slab Furnace and a Sifting Table, used to get mineral materials and more from Dirt, Gravel, Sand and Dust (Dust!) blocks.

# Agrarian Skies

**Installed through:** Feed the Beast Launcher
**Minecraft Version Compatible:** Automatic
**Link:** bit.ly/FTBLauncherLink

Mods are awesome: that, we think most everyone would agree on. However, since mods add so much new stuff and change up the game so extensively, it can be super overwhelming to fire one up and see all this new stuff you don't know how to mess with. Many mods come with little in-game Books that you can open up and read, but trying to remember all the things you read and switching back and forth between them and actually playing is pretty darn hard, even for the best Crafters.

That's why we suggest that, if you're looking to actually learn how to do some of the amazing things in mods like all of the Tinkers' mods, Thaumcraft, Thermal Expansion or Applied Energistics, check out the Agrarian Skies modpack. Actually a super, super modded version of Skyblock (see the Mini-Games section) and available on the FTB Launcher, Agrarian Skies puts you in a world where you have very little to start with, but all of the things you need to eventually build everything in the mods. It uses a very well-done and inventive questing system to teach you how to do a ton of the stuff in these mods by making them goals, and it does so in a way that's both hugely entertaining and also quite challenging. If we had to pick, Agrarian Skies would be our very favorite modpack of all.

Pixelmon contains almost all of your favorite Pokémon, just wandering around and waiting to be captured.

# Pixelmon

**Installed through:** Technic Launcher
**Minecraft Version Compatible:** Automatic
**Link:** bit.ly/TechnicPixelmon

It's no secret that Pokémon is one of the most popular and long-lasting game series of all time, so that the hardcore modding community for Minecraft has gone out and recreated Pokémon inside of their own game is no big shock to anyone. Pixelmon is just that modpack, and to answer your questions: Yes, there are Pokémon wandering around; yes, you can catch them; yes, you can fight them with trainers and other players; and yes, it all works.

Though you can just load this one up through the Feed the Beast launcher and play in your own world, we'd also suggest jumping on one of the official servers (just go to multiplayer instead of single player, and they're listed) where people have actually gone so far as to build functioning Pokémon Centers, gyms and even the Elite Four! Plus, you can show off your sick Mewtwo and find hundreds of other players to battle with. This one's a treat, whether you're a longtime Pokémon fan or just like the idea of a bunch of adorable battle creatures wandering around your Minecraft home.

# The Minecraft Challenge List

Looking for something to do in Minecraft today? See how many of these challenges you can complete, and keep track of your score! Even more fun if you can compete with your friends, and no cheatin'!

## Easy (10 pts)

- Dig a 20x20 pit all the way to the Bedrock
- Create a solid Block of each type of ore (Expert Bonus for 50 pts, create a house out of Blocks of Diamond!)
- Build a Nether home
- Build a moat all the way around your house out of Water or Lava
- Create a Redstone Piston trapdoor in front of your base's entrance -or- create an automatic double Iron Door entrance that fires at the same time
- Win a round of Spleef!
- Make a "lavacast" by getting up very high and pouring Water over Lava. Looks super cool and makes a giant structure!
- Install and play 2 mods with different modloaders
- Download a map from online and explore it

# Intermediate (20 pts)

- Get a Skeleton to kill a Creeper
- Screenshot the hardest to find mobs in vanilla Minecraft: A Spider Jockey, a Charged Creeper and a Wither
- Kill an Enderman with only Water
- Build a custom Spleef! arena
- Find all three Strongholds on a Map
- Win a match of UHC
- Craft one of every kind of potion
- Build a tower from the Bedrock to the sky limit
- "Beat" the game
- Download an Adventure mode map from online and complete the adventure

# Hard (35 pts)

- Find and clear out an Abandoned Mineshaft without Diamond Armor or Diamond weapons and with no enchantments or potions
- Defeat one of every kind of mob, including the Wither and the Ender Dragon
- Build an automated Wheat farm that will grow 20 Wheat with Bonemeal, harvest it, move it to a Hopper, push it into a Minecart with Chest and move it to another Hopper in your base that deposits it in a Chest
- Kill enough Creepers to make a full stack of TNT
- Craft a set of Diamond Armor with all Level V enchantments and a Diamond Sword with all Level V enchantments

# All New Gallery!

With each edition of our Minecraft books, we bring you a gallery of images featuring some of the best builds we've come across in our long journey through the many realms of Minecraft. For this publication, we decided to go very current with most of our choices, picking builds that were not only gorgeous and worthy of praise, but which also were released in the days just around the writing of the book itself, with the exception of a few that we thought were just too good to not include.

Because of that, it's unlikely that even the most well-traveled Crafters out there have seen many of these maps! On top of that, this just shows how strong the Minecraft creative community is running these days, and that there are endless reservoirs of creativity out there still to tap. **Enjoy!**

Curves can be really hard to pull off well in Minecraft, but these not only look great, they look quite life-like in terms of architecture.

# A Thai Themed Jungle Map

**by Whisper974**

Created for PVP, the idyllic setting of this delicate temple in the jungle will play nicely off of the sights and sounds of combat. Whisper974 says the inspiration came from eating in a Thai restaurant, which is a nice reminder that the concept for a build can come from just about anywhere. Beyond just building the temple itself, the landscape around the temple was also crafted to give the setting some extra oomph, and Whisper974 says the trees were designed by Crafter monsterfish. Don't they just look great?

# Avaricia

**by Schnogot**

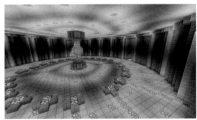

Another architecturally sound build, Avaricia is one that shows just what shaders can do to a room that's well-lit.

Some builders just know how to balance color, even with the limited palette that Minecraft provides us, and Schnogot is one of those builders. Also impressive for this build that was done for an arena contest is the efficiency and balance of the architecture, with nothing in this build looking even a block out of place. This build is not just about looks though, as it is designed to feature survival combat, with multiple areas with different aesthetics to battle over.

# AWESOME
## Minecraft hub

**by TheRoyalPixels**

Hubs like this are used in online servers like the ones in our Spotlight chapter, and this one is a perfect balance of accessible and gorgeously designed.

Hubs are a big part of the world of Minecraft servers, as they serve as access points to mini-games and server sections. Designing hubs is a major medium in the Minecraft world, as the hub is what every player that joins a server sees, making it the calling card and a mark of quality for the server. Here TheRoyalPixels have knocked a hub out of the proverbial park; note the the spaces left for mini-game names, the mark of a hub map.

# Norbert—The Bear

**by moustafa74**

Ol' Norbert is lookin' like he might just reach down and snatch up a miner or two for a snack!

While buildings are by far the most common subject of Minecraft creations, sometimes it's nice to be reminded that our favorite blocky builder is capable of many creations beyond those architectural ones. Norbert is one such example- a mighty bear reaching 200 blocks into the sky, which creator moustafa74 says took him a few hours to get the curves down on. Creations like this often find their way into bigger maps, as players can insert them using special tools like the ones mentioned in our software section of this book.

History is one of the best places to go for Minecraft build inspiration. Grab a few images online, or get yourself a classic architecture book, and try incorporating something you see into your build. This will give your creations flair and details that you might not have thought of otherwise.

# Castellum Romanorum

**by edsinger**

Another hub, this is one with a bit of a historical architecture theme. We're reminded in this build of the glory days of the great civilizations of the past, seeing a building that would fit easily into a fantasy world's history book, but which has yet to fall into ruins and is in pristine condition. The little touches on this map elevate it from simply good to gorgeous, such as the geometric shapes cut into the sides of the towers and the neat details of the underwater columns. Great work, edsinger!

Worlds like Cave Settlement that restrict themselves to a smaller area are really fun to explore, and can also provide quite the Survival challenge.

# Cave Settlement

## by JelleB14

Cave Settlement was created to give its builder, JelleB14, a challenge. Having played on creative servers online, where individual plots are handed out to builders, JelleB14 had grown tired of building on the massive plots that they have available to them as a skilled builder. For Cave Settlement, Jelle decided to go with a very small plot and build to the sky limit. Instead of trying to fit a skinny tower or some such in, JelleB14 instead made this amazing "cutaway" build, which features a whole settlement woven through the caves of this column of rock. This idea of setting limits on oneself in order to push creative boundaries is something that artists in many mediums in mediums outside of Minecraft do, and it is one of the best ways to come up with new creative thoughts you would not otherwise have had.

That this map is built not only to look great, but also contains an extensive Survival mode challenge is a true feat of creation. It's also very impressive that this build manages to be so balanced and symmetrical, as a real airship would need to be, yet it has so much variety of detail.

# Cloud Haven

**by lynchinc**

You didn't think we'd let a book go by without a bit of a steampunk ship build, did'ya? Not on our watch! This cityship is called Cloud Haven, and its background story is that it once was part of a mining operation, sailing across the world and mining anti-gravity materials from islands floating in the skies. Calamity then hit the world of the ship, forcing all inhabitants to take to the skies to survive, which meant Cloud Haven was recommissioned as a cityship that can hold upwards of 1000 "traders, skylords, merchants, smugglers, pirates and proletariat alike," as creator lynchinc puts it. Not content just to build an amazing ship, lynch also made this a Survival challenge map, with the idea being that the player has to explore the ship to find things to survive, trading with the villagers and hunting for the secret Treasury Room, with the eventual goal being to build a house on a nearby island. Creative, challenging and a great all-around map.

# Contemporary Museum

**by Joueur_inconnu**

Joueur_inconnu is a builder who has almost certainly studied the architecture of real-world contemporary art museums, because their rendition of one is so spot on that it almost looks real. Even conceptually, this build is excellent, as the old-world aqueduct-esque arches in the front of the museum provide a thought-provoking contrast to the straight lines and unabashed modernity of the rest of the structure. This build is also interesting when you compare it to the next, Courtmere Palace, as it barely looks like they were made in the same game. That's the power of the versatility of Minecraft, and the skill that a builder like Joueur_inconnu has.

Shaders really make the Contemporary Museum's perfect minimal design shine.

# Courtmere Palace

### by DJpaulii

Part of the Teweran server, DJpaulii built this towering and graceful structure after being inspired by the town hall in the city of Vienna. DJpaulii is one of those crafters whose creative skills are bolstered by a knowledge of true, real-life architectural concepts, such as arches and buttresses. This kind of knowledge is what you should seek if you find yourself loving builds like this one, where the detail is tremendous and masterfully executed. In fact, if creating buildings of staggering detail is something you're passionate about, you might want to consider making architecture your career!

It's hard to give a sense of just how massive Courtmere Palace is from these images. What's more impressive, perhaps, than its size, however, is that it still is about a 1:1 ratio, meaning as a player the building is about the size it would be in real life. It's really hard to get this much detail into a 1:1 building, so much kudos to DJpaulii.

# Dunyazade Oasis Home

**by Tech Zero**

Dunyazade looks good at all times of day, and is a home we'd gladly make our own in the real world.

If you ever find yourself building the same old houses over and over again, and you just can't think of a new detail to add or a concept to play with, get online and find yourself some builds like this one from Tech Zero to play in. Here, Tech Zero starts with the concept of a desert house as a jumping off point, and where they end up is someplace unique and unlike any house we've seen before. It's not tremendously big, resembling more the home of a real person than the palaces we so often see, and it has a combination of traditional desert architecture form the past and a new, contemporary housing style that blends together perfectly. And those sails to keep the sun off are just a touch of genius.

# Frosty the Snowman

**by _themineman23_**

Something's definitely changed about Frosty from his days as a cartoon to this towering, hungry-lookin' iteration.

Building something architecturally amazing or conceptually technical is great, and we love builds like that, but sometimes the most fun you can have with a build is just to let go and do something crazy and wild. For instance, a giant evil snowman! Frosty here looks ready to kill, and it's not hard to imagine that _themineman23_ was having a lot of fun when he brought this monster to life.

Sometimes using just one color or even type of block can be done in a way that makes for beautiful builds. It's all about shape, when you go mono-color, and this build has some lovely shapes indeed.

# Gallifrey Citadel

**by themixedt4pe**

Some of you might recognize the name Gallifrey as the moniker for the planet in *Doctor Who* from which the famous Time Lords come from. This cool spherical castle build is based on that very concept, and it shows what a builder can do with a palette of just a few types of blocks. This build also highlights once again that taking the time to handcraft the natural environment around the build is often key to a build going from cool to incredible.

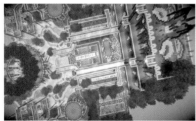

Another super-massive build, the Hanging Gardens is all the more impressive for being built by just one player. Planning alone would be a huge undertaking!

# Hanging Gardens of Azyros

**by Pikipikipuku**

Now this is a big 'un, with buckets of detail and a perfectly executed concept. It feels as you go about this enormous build that you are a jungle explorer stepping foot into a previously undiscovered ancient ruin in near pristine condition, and a bigger one than has ever been found before. Made for the mixnets server, this build took Pikipikipuku 4 months to build all on their own, and we think it was time spent in a fully worthwhile pursuit.

# Infamous

**by NewHeaven**

Every book, we include at least one map of a city that is so big, even we have barely scratched the surface of exploring it. For this one, it's Infamous by NewHeaven—over a dozen people spent time on this behemoth, creating a city that feels both real due to its level of detail and also completely fantastical, as it's fully realized. This is one that we highly recommend heading to PlanetMinecraft and downloading to do a bit of personal exploring on. A tremendous, stunning effort all around.

In taking images for this book, we did not even explore a small fraction of this massive city, despite an hour or so walking its streets and flying over its many neighborhoods. This could make a great map to try and survive in, giving your Survival mode an urban, post-apocalyptic kinda feel.

# Kelestria

**by MrPorteEnBois**

If Courtmere Palace looks like a structure right off the street of a real-life city, Kelestria looks like something from a fantasy novel brought to life. This palace has a cool backstory as well, being the last known above-water location in a world that was punished for refusing to live in harmony with nature. Kelestria is the location where the last good men were allowed to go and live, in the magnificent palace crowning the final island floating above the sea.

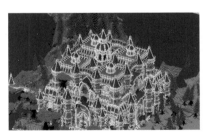

One thing you can't tell from these images is that the island that Kelestria is on is rather huge itself, and it is hand-designed. This attention to detail, building up the background that might not even be seen by any other players, helps to give weight to the narrative of a build, making it feel like a real place.

# Medieval Build Contest World

## by BebopVox

Not all medieval cities are created equal, and few can hope to rival this contest submission by BebopVox for personality and detail. Though the town remains void of people, one can just imagine them going about their complex lives in this town that has everything from a keep to a village to a graveyard and even a gallows. This build also plays with the idea of fantasy without overdoing it, showing us that there are many paths available out there for builds that can blur the line between fantastical and realistic.

Online build contests on sites like Planet Minecraft often result in some of the best builds ever done in Minecraft. If you're looking for a challenge and a little exposure, head to PM and watch for the next big contest; they're a great way to get your builds out there and expand your abilities.

# Oasis of the Seas at Terminal 18

## by CharlesGoldburn

Many people build boat replicas, few do them on a 1:1 scale, and even fewer make those boats seem completely alive with details both inside and out. This very recent build by CharlesGoldburn is a recreation of the world's largest cruise ship, and each of its seven neighborhoods inside are fully explorable! At 362 blocks long (1187 ft), this entertainment titan can hold up to 6360 passengers and 2394 crew at the same time, making it bigger than many small towns.

Doing a recreation of a real-world (or even a fantasy-world) boat or ship is nothing new, but this one is special. Not only is it a 1:1 of the largest cruise ship in the world, making it the largest cruise ship Minecraft recreation as well, it's also perfectly detailed. The entire thing is recreated, inside and out, and it really feels like a cruise ship. Downright perfection on the part of CharlesGoldburn.

**81**

# P.I.E: Plant Investigation Experiments

**by VigourBuilds**

We love it when a builder takes the time to not only craft a very cool and unique structure, but also to do so based around a story concept they entirely created themselves. This is just what VigourBuilds accomplished with P.I.E., which is actually a giant machine that is moved about the world to test plants all over in order to find cures for a disease or to find plants that can help humanity have enough oxygen on a spaceship to leave Earth. The enormous machine is crewed by 6 people and 15 mini helicopters, and it stays in each location for about 10 years before being shifted to another hopeful spot.

One can just envision the intrepid scientists working in this monstrosity to save the planet.

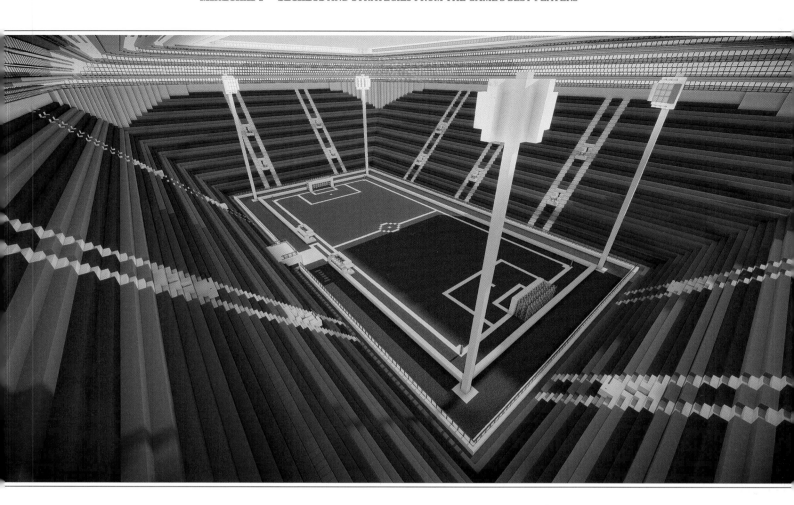

# Stadium

**by Roux**

Stadiums are common choices for builds in Minecraft, but this one truly stands out as a triumph of a concept brought to life. Many stadiums end up as simple giant boxes that fulfill the necessary requirements to be called such, but not Roux's, which has architectural flair as well as attention to real-world details. It feels like a team is just about to run onto the pitch as you look at it, something that's hard to achieve in this game that often looks so different from reality.

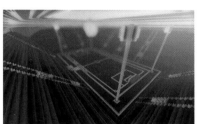

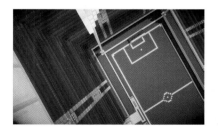

The details like the massive light poles, the detailing on the semi-enclosed roof, the curved corners of the structure and the entrance and exit tunnels make this one of the best stadiums we've ever seen in Minecraft.

# Teweran Survival Games 3

**by the Teweran**

Created by a group of builders from one of the world's most excellent servers, this creation is meant to host a match of one of Minecraft's most popular mini-games, the Survival Games. It's currently located on The Hive server (hivemc.us), and it is meant to be the setting for a truly epic, multi-day match between competitors. The city itself is big enough, with dozens of layers and buildings and hidey spots, but this map also contains a very well-incorporated natural section as well, making it perhaps the best Survival Games map we've ever seen.

Few maps are this detailed, much less ones that are made for Survival Games matches. It has a fully-realized aesthetic and concept, feeling like a city you'd see as a central location in anime or a sci-fi novel.

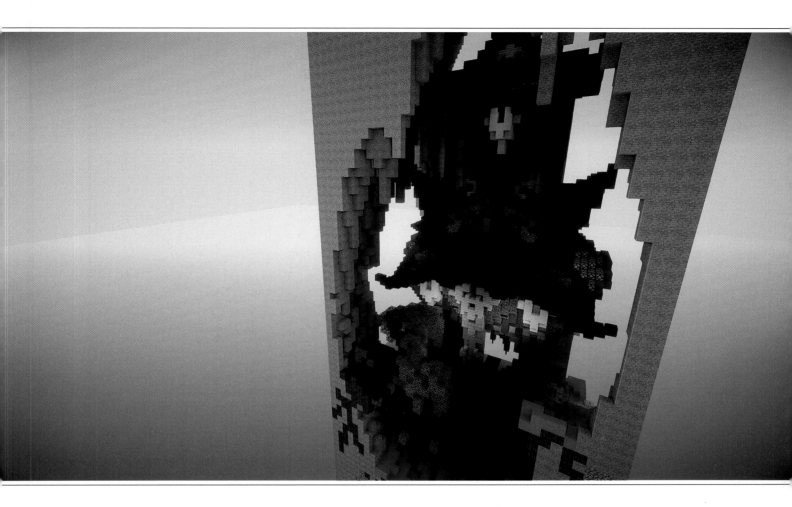

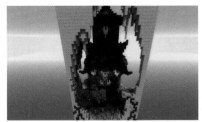

Yet another example of the rule that builds don't have to be huge to be well-done and highly creative, axewemolga's temple is a lesson in efficiency and thinking outside of the box, this time by thinking inside of it.

# Vasovenular Interna

**by axewemolga**

Another example of the ultra-cool "cutaway" style of build, this one is a slightly Asian-influenced temple bursting forth from a solid block of stone. Another build that was first created on an online creative server with personal plots, we think it's notable for its willingness to take from real-life architecture while flipping and twisting those ideas into an aesthetic all its own. Note the thoughtful use of colors, of which it uses many, but all of which flow together without clashing. The idea of making it beautiful and earthy while also including dark elements like skulls gives this temple a personalized feel; one can almost see the world it originated from in their mind.

# Minecraft, YouTube and a New Kind of Star:

## An Interview with TheDiamondMinecart

Daniel "TheDiamondMinecart" Middleton • YouTube Creator

Here we see TDM in his custom skin along with his popular video characters Dr. Trayaurus and his skeleton dog Grim.

# YouTube is the future of entertainment.

More than movies, more than TV, more than music, the world of YouTube channels and the hugely popular personalities that run them is one of the fastest growing entertainment forms in the world. In fact, according to a poll taken by Variety magazine, teenagers are now far more likely to recognize YouTube stars than they are the most famous actors in the world (the most-recognized non-YouTuber, Paul Walker, came in at a distant 6th place in the poll).

To put it even more into perspective, the videos YouTube stars make on their channels often out-do huge music videos and movie trailers to become the most watched things on YouTube, and the medium racks up many billions of views every month. That's right: billions, and it's not all just for fun either. Through the ads program which shows advertisements before or alongside videos, YouTube channel-runners are able to make actual money from their videos. When those videos start to earn thousands, then millions of views, they earn more money with every view, making YouTube channels not only quite popular, but quite lucrative as well.

Much of what these suddenly super-famous YouTube stars focus on in their videos is that other titan of the "new" entertainment, video gaming. Particularly, stars upload sessions of themselves playing and reacting to their favorite games in a genre of video know as the Let's Play, a phenomenon in its own right that sits within the overall YouTube phenomenon.

Daniel Middleton is one such YouTuber who has combined this idea of Let's Play YouTube videos with the world's most popular video game, Minecraft. His channel is called TheDiamondMinecart (https://www.youtube.com/user/TheDiamondMinecart), and on it he uploads Let's Plays of Minecraft just about every day. TheDiamondMinecart, or TDM, has a very large following, with 15+ videos with over 5 million views, 200+ with over 1 million, and as of the writing of this book, 3,349,246 subscribers to his channel on YouTube.

That last number is more people than live in the city of Chicago by about 500k. To call it impressive is to understate massively, but how does this all work? What exactly do YouTubers like Dan do, and how does it get so popular?

We asked Dan to describe the YouTube channel-runner's job, and this is how he put it: "My job consists of using my imagination for cool new video ideas, recording those ideas within Minecraft (and sometimes other games too!), taking those recordings and editing them together to create the final piece and then creating the artwork to go with the video when it goes live on YouTube." Though to the casual viewer it may look similar to regular gaming, Dan says that there's a lot more to it than that, adding "I do get to play and record video games every day, but there's also a lot of behind-the-scenes, too."

Anyone can start a YouTube channel with just a few clicks, but it takes gaming know-how, special recording equipment (such as high fidelity microphones and powerful video capture software), passion, dedication and not just a little charisma to gain a following like that of Dan and his fellow YouTube stars. As he says, it doesn't happen overnight, but took months of work and practice before he really hit a chord with viewers and his channel took off. "I would say my first big break was over the summer of 2013. I had been making Minecraft videos everyday for a few months, but when the summer hit and I started showcasing Mods for the game and bringing my own stories into those videos, people seemed to really connect with them and it has got me to where I am today."

The 22 year-old says that his channel's growth from a small following to his millions of subscribers happened "Very quick!" adding "I literally just finished my university degree and education as a whole and over the summer, the YouTube channel exploded." But in one way it's no surprise that he'd fit so well into the Let's Play world. Dan is and always has been a passionate gamer, telling us, "I have always been a huge fan of video games, playing since I was very young, all the way up until now. They have always been a big part of my life; I have dabbled in video game design, digital art, animation and

simply just playing games while going through education, and the website YouTube gives me the perfect platform to show my video creations to the world."

With gaming being bigger than it ever has been, it's the ideal time for game-based YouTubers to make their mark, and Dan believes things are only going to get bigger for video games. "I think the gaming industry is really at a peak right now with the Internet being so powerful in the creation and growth of video games," he said. "You don't have to be a big developer with a huge team any more to create a smash hit game, just an idea and the passion to put it together, just like with Minecraft.

I'd say the industry will continue to grow with the importance of the internet and I also think eSports are another huge way of getting gaming out to the masses."

For those who think YouTube Creator sounds like a fun job, Dan has a lot of encouraging advice, telling kids who are looking to start their own channel, "Make sure you're having fun doing what you do. If you aren't having fun making a video, your viewers will be able to tell. So as long as you are having fun doing YouTube then keep at it! Getting popular doesn't happen overnight so be patient, and maybe you'll find one of your great creations go far!"

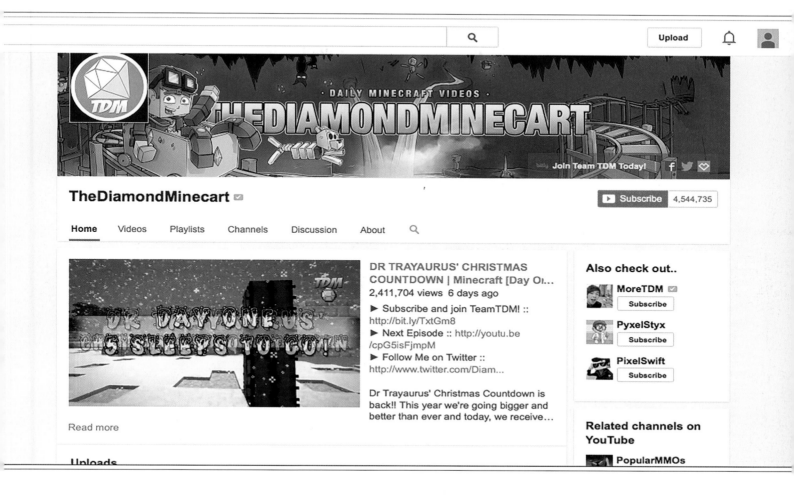

And don't worry if you don't know what you're doing right away; Dan learned his skills on the job! "The whole process of starting a YouTube channel with limited knowledge of how it works and the programs/games you are working with is really fascinating, so starting from knowing everything really wouldn't be the same. The best part of being a YouTuber is that you can create whatever you want, while learning new skills all the time."

Though it only takes one look at a TheDiamondMinecart video to see that Dan is a young man with heaps of both talent and personality, he is nothing but humble and appreciative about his success, telling

us, "I am very privileged to be able to have [TheDiamondMinecart] as my full time job."

Whether you're a gamer, have another interest or simply want to talk to the world, YouTube is a place where you can start sharing your thoughts with almost no set up and at no cost, making it one of the most accessible entertainment industries in history. All you need is a free channel, a way to record, a little software, an idea, and some time. And who knows? You might just be the next YouTube star that all the kids are talking about. ∎

Douche Canoe 2

# Other Building Games

As is tradition with our other books, this is our chapter all about spreading the love of building and sandbox style games to other titles. While Minecraft might be the reigning king of builders, and without a doubt one of the most excellent survival titles in existence, it is far from the only entry in either of these genres, and there are some seriously excellent games out there that we think Crafters might find pretty darn fun as well.

Now, this list is far from exhaustive; we've just chosen a few of the games that fit into a variety of genres and styles related to Minecraft to give you an

Building games come in all shapes and looks, not to mention levels of complexity!

overview of what's been created in these genres. There are many more great sandbox games, voxel games and builder games in the world, but these are just a few of our favorites. If any of these seem like something you'd like to play, they're all available online for pretty darn cheap, and we'd highly recommend giving one or two a whirl if you love Minecraft.

# Ace of Spades

**aceofspades.com**

**How it's like Minecraft:** Features voxel graphics and destructible/buildable terrain, but in a first person multiplayer shooter.

*Ace of Spades* is a wild little shooter that allows players to interact with the environment similarly to Minecraft, in that you can destroy just about anything you see and can build structures on the fly. Think Minecraft's building combined with *Team Fortress 2's* combat. It's a pretty small game, made by an indie studio, and the graphics are nothing to write home about, but in terms of ingenuity and gameplay, it's a heck of a title.

As an example: imagine that you and your team are holed up in a tower, being shot at by enemies from below. Normally in an FPS you'd have to risk peeking out the windows or running out the doors, which are known points and will surely be covered. In *Ace*

*Ace of Spades* maps and modes have a great look that, while owing something to Minecraft, are all their own.

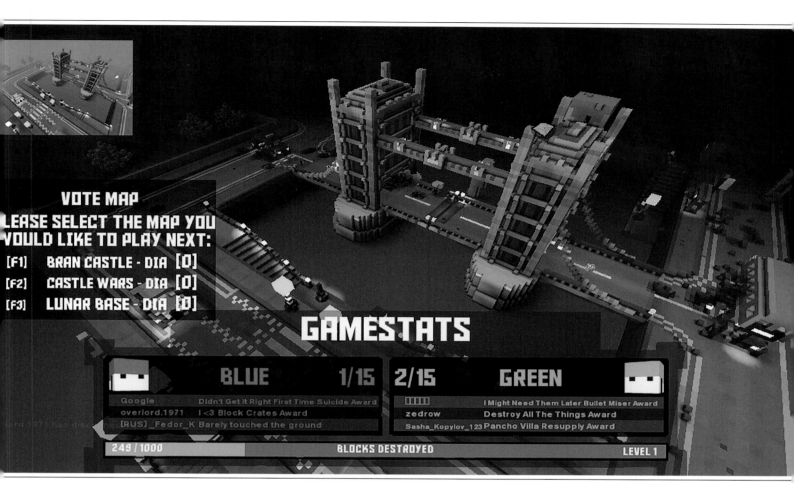

VOTE MAP

LEASE SELECT THE MAP YOU
VOULD LIKE TO PLAY NEXT:

[F1]    BRAN CASTLE - DIA [0]

[F2]    CASTLE WARS - DIA [0]

[F3]    LUNAR BASE - DIA [0]

GAMESTATS

| | BLUE | 1/15 | 2/15 | GREEN | |
|---|---|---|---|---|---|
| Google | Didn't Get It Right First Time Suicide Award | | | I Might Need Them Later Bullet Miser Award | |
| overlord.1971 | I <3 Block Crates Award | | zedrow | Destroy All The Things Award | |
| [RUS]_Fedor_K | Barely touched the ground | | Sasha_Kopylov_123 | Pancho Villa Resupply Award | |

249 / 1000    BLOCKS DESTROYED    LEVEL 1

*Ace of Spades* doesn't have the huge following of Minecraft, but its community is dedicated and there are always players online to battle with.

*of Spades,* you have other options. You could punch a hole in a wall with a shovel, creating a new spot to snipe from, or you could tunnel down from the tower and out, maybe even coming up behind the enemy! You could also use your building skills to add more fortifications to the tower or block the enemy's view to your doorway, giving you the cover you need to get out and kick butt.

*Ace of Spades'* voxel-based landscape and low graphics needs allows for a lot of freedom, not only in terms of player strategy, but also in the physical design of levels and game modes. The developers have obviously become quite skilled at using their own tools, and many of the levels in *Ace of Spades* rival Minecraft builds in terms of detail and creative design. You also get to play in awesome modes like the Zombie mode, where one player begins as a zombie and attempts to infect all other players, turning the tide of battle one infection at a time.

Big, big updates are in the works for *Starbound* according to its creators. One from around the turn of 2015 features a revamped questing mode as well as a whole new race to play, the Novakids. Who knows what's next!

# Starbound

**playstarbound.com**

**How it's like Minecraft:** Imagine Minecraft as a side-scroller, with more combat and item variation, and in space! That's basically *Starbound*.

The sister game to the most famous side-scroller Minecraft-esque game, *Terraria*, *Starbound* takes the idea of mining, building and crafting and puts it into a space-y, adventure-filled future. *Starbound* is set to get some major updates going forward, where *Terraria's* run of updates is at an end, thus why we include this spacefaring builder and not its more famous sibling.

The premise of *Starbound* is one of the most exciting in games for those who have always dreamed of exploring the stars: you create a quite customized character (in terms of appearance) that is one of seven different distinct races, and you have your own personal spaceship that you can use to travel between different planetary systems.

Each race has a very particular aesthetic, from the robotic Glitch to the birdlike Avians, as does each planet you visit. Here's where *Starbound* excels: instead of biomes like in Minecraft, you have planets that each have their own particular environment, materials, wildlife and people living on them (or not). They look entirely different one to the next, and even have differing weather systems, temperatures and danger levels.

The level of customization between each planet and each character is only expanded by the absolutely staggering variety of items that are available in *Starbound,* where there are dozens of different types of dirt, stone and sand alone, not to mention a system of randomized weapons that rivals *Borderlands* games in its variety, and quite a few more mob types than Minecraft.

In many ways the game is very similar to Minecraft- you explore, dig, look for ore, smelt it,

make tools, craft items, find more items to craft better things with, there's a night and day cycle and building a base is very important. However, there are some major differences, besides the side-scrolling view and the cute sprite-based art style. The combat and movement in Starbound are a lot more straightforward and less complex than Minecraft, which might be considered good by some people and bad by others. The landscapes of each planet are more uniform than a Minecraft world, but there's far more variety between planets than between Minecraft biomes. Additionally, bosses and a quest line are more central to Starbound than in Minecraft, where they're essentially optional.

This game, as mentioned, is continuously being updated for free (after initial purchase), so if you love Minecraft and think something with a bit more aesthetic flair and adventure-focus would be fun, now is a great time to get into *Starbound*.

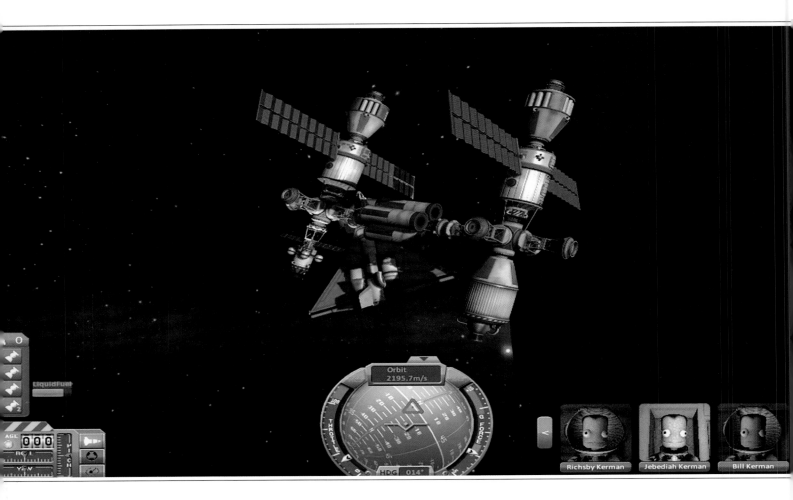

*KSP* has a special place in the hearts of many indie game fans for its perfect meshing of a lighthearted, experiment-encouraging design and some of the hardest, most technical gameplay you'll ever come across.

# Kerbal Space Program

**kerbalspaceprogram.com**

**How it's like Minecraft:** It's all about piecing things together and trying new builds. Though there's not the same kind of first-person free-roam experience, Kerbal's system of building and low-res graphics scratch the same itch that Redstone engineering or creating complex buildings can in Minecraft.

**Note:** There was a major update to *Kerbal Space Program* just as this book was going to print, so some of the images here are out of date. That's a good thing, because there's more to do in this game now, and it was already super fun!

Kerbals! They're teeny, they're green, they're adorable goofballs, and they just wanna go to space. *Kerbal Space Program,* or *KSP,* is a game all about building rockets and other vehicles to put these little green guys up through their planet's atmosphere and beyond. Your job is to design the ships that take them there and the vehicles they use when they get where they're going, whether that's a

shuttle to go to a space station or a lander that'll set down on a planet and drop a little rover off.

All of this is done through a very fun system of quests and resource-acquiring, which is tied into the missions that you undertake. Do well in your missions and achieve the goals set in front of you, and you'll unlock more parts to build cooler rockets and ships and other vehicles. Each Kerbal astronaut you have gets a history and skills as well, and you can follow their teeny careers as you expand Kerbal reach into space.

Doing that, though- actually getting Kerbals into space and back alive- is not an easy task. In fact, we'd say that this game is really for those who have a deep love for astronomy, rocketships and aeronautics, engineering or all three. That's not to say it's not fun for most people to play, it's just really complex and hard to master. Essentially, it's a very cute-looking thing that's a game on the

surface, but in reality is a rocketship construction and flight simulator. You'll tangle with weight distribution and centers of thrust, nudging rockets into correct orbits, aerodynamics and many more hard science issues as you play Kerbal, making it a game that some will absolutely love the challenge of, and one that some will find far too imposing to play for more than an hour or so.

If Redstone's complexity scares you off, you might want to look elsewhere, but if a technical challenge that's also a very fun and quirky game is your jam, this is the game for you. Few accomplishments in games feel as satisfying as getting a self-designed rocket up into space successfully, and few games are so hilarious when everything just goes totally wrong. Those poor little Kerbals do have a tendency to get blown up…

# Roblox

**roblox.com**

**How it's like Minecraft:** A voxel-building game with a heavy focus on multiplayer, though without the world generation features. More focused on creating levels and mini-games to play, there is no survival mode.

*Roblox* is unique in a few ways, the primary of which are that it's totally free and that it's aimed at kids between 8 and 18. The idea of *Roblox* is that you take control of an avatar in a voxel world and explore and play in creations made by yourself and others. Unlike Minecraft, there's no set survival or "vanilla" type mode; worlds are created from the ground up and then are shared on the primary *Roblox* website by users.

Another difference between Minecraft and *Roblox* is that you design worlds in *Roblox* using an editor, much like MCEdit or one of the other out of game editors available for Minecraft. There is construction in the game itself, if the world is set up to do so, but it's more about creating a scenario to play in than it is about warping a world as you play.

*Roblox* also offers a lot more options in terms of how you can create, with "bricks" of many different sizes, customizable character body models and a pretty huge amount of readymade items to include

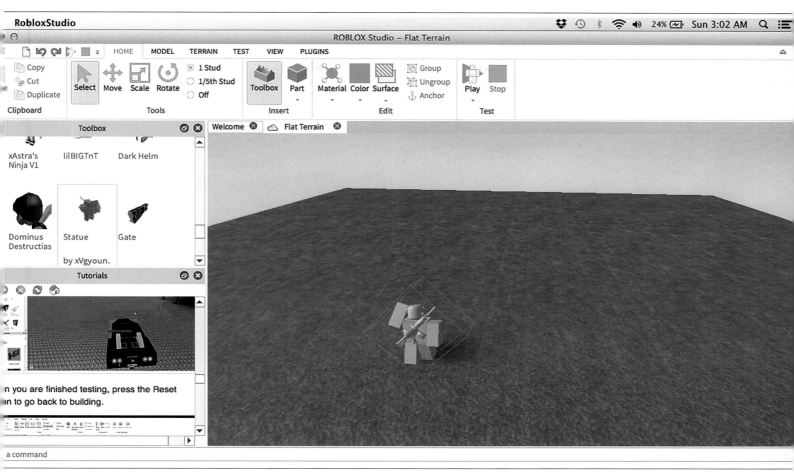

A shot of the *Roblox* builder, with which players can create just about any scenario they can think up.

in your worlds. There's even a "lightweight" programming language, Lua, that players can use to script events and further customize the worlds that they build. It's pretty heady to start off with, but being designed for kids, *Roblox* is set up to teach you how to use itself. In fact, it's a pretty excellent tool for getting kids interested in coding, and a fun way to learn real-world applicable skills.

*Roblox* is all about community, with the aforementioned website being the hub of most activity in the game. It also includes a static currency, giving players incentive to travel to different worlds and complete activities, all of which feed back into their ability to do more with their own worlds and characters.

*Roblox* is certainly complicated enough for adults, but where it shines is in being an excellent online destination for kids that's both fun and intellectually stimulating. If you're a youngin', or a parent of a youngin', that wants a more kid-friendly version of Minecraft that's less about survival and more about the building, definitely give *Roblox* a good look.

YOU SURVIVED FOR 5 HOURS.

# Project Zomboid

**projectzomboid.com**

**How it's like Minecraft:** Survival in a sandbox world kicked up to the max, with the expectation of death, plus a good amount of item hunting and crafting, with a little building thrown in.

On the opposite end of both the kid-friendly spectrum and the creation-focused spectrum from *Roblox* is the harrowing and stressful zombie survival game *Project Zomboid*. You won't be doing much building in *PZ*, except to board up windows and doors to keep the walkers out, but what you certainly will be doing is desperately fending off hunger, depression, panic, illness and thirst as you struggle to survive in a world overrun by zombie hordes.

A game that's still in early-access, meaning it's not complete yet, *PZ* is one of the most promising survival games and zombie games out right now. While it's still getting many of the kinks worked out and features implemented, what is complete of this game is already super exciting to play.

Like Minecraft inspiration *Dwarf Fortress*, *Project Zomboid* is a game where the question isn't when you will lose, it's how and how much fun it was to do so.

In *Project Zomboid* you are a user-created character that finds themselves the only survivor in the Hardin and Meade County areas of Kentucky. The game is designed after real-life locations in the counties, including the towns of Muldraugh and West Point, and you have to navigate the giant, zombie-infested area trying to gather enough supplies to survive.

*PZ* does not make this easy. In fact, it's almost impossible. Everything is measured in *PZ*, down to your levels of stress and panic, your blood amount, what parts of your body are damaged and how, and every action is recorded and causes a giant skill pool to be upgraded. At first it seems easy, but as you run out of supplies in the area around your spawn point, you will quickly have to move on to other areas, and you risk major injury or worse every time you set foot outside of a house. You're not even safe in houses, to be frank. And this is all not to even mention how hard it gets when the electricity and water shut off after a random amount of time.

*PZ* is a game that will kill you, but that very level of danger, stress and simulation is what gives it such a strong draw. While, like *Kerbal Space Program*, it's not a game for people who want simple, easy fun, those who wish the survival part of Minecraft was a little more complex and challenging will eat this one up.

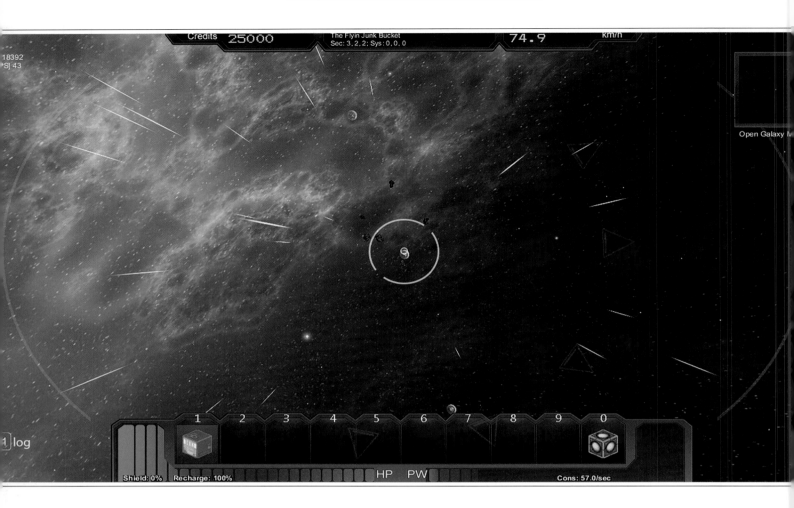

# StarMade

**star-made.org**

**How it's like Minecraft:** Block-based builder like Minecraft with a focus on spaceships like *Kerbal Space Program,* but much less punishing and with a first-person, exploration angle.

Take the space focus of *Starbound,* add the first-person voxel exploration and crafting of Minecraft and the spaceship design idea of *Kerbal Space Program,* and you get the indie game *StarMade.* While not as polished as any of those three, StarMade is also not as punishing or hard to pick up, and it does an excellent job of combining the things that make those games fun into something all its own.

Another early access game, *StarMade* puts the player into a vast universe as an astronaut with the ability to mine the worlds, asteroids and other space-faring objects around them, turning them into whatever kind of ship they'd like to fly about in. It also features space stations, factions, planets you can fly straight up

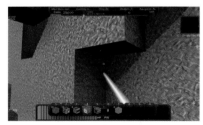

The planet you can see in the bottom image here must be flown to from far across the galaxy and is one of many such planets in the game.

A surface shot of the planet from page 104, each planet actually has its own resources and even gravity, which doesn't activate until you get close.

to, land on and walk about and even guns (something only possible in Minecraft with mods).

The galaxy of *StarMade* truly is vast and fully explorable, and unlike *Kerbal's* shipbuilding system that uses pre-made pieces, or the hand-drawn ships of Starbound, the customization level for spaceships in *StarMade* is truly extreme. If you can think of how to make it happen with blocks and the other many small pieces available in *StarMade,* you can build it in the game.

It truly is the only game that can be justifiably called Minecraft in space at this point, and though it's still pretty rough, it has a ton of potential. Oh, and it's totally free to play as of December 2014, which means there's very little reason not to try it out.

This is a free excerpt from our new book *The Ultimate Guide to Mastering Circuit Power!: Minecraft®™ Redstone and the Keys to Supercharging Your Builds in Sandbox Games.* This will get you started on learning Redstone; to learn more, look for *The Ultimate Guide to Mastering Circuit Power!: Minecraft®™ Redstone and the Keys to Supercharging Your Builds in Sandbox Games* at a retail store near you or online!

# The Basics

Ready to start your journey to becoming a master of all that is Redstone? Well then, let's dive right on in and get familiar with the basics of the Redstone world! Before we do so, however, lets talk for a moment about how to best use this book to get the most out of it and to become the most knowledgable Redstone engineer you can:

# How to Use This Book

Redstone is a massive topic, almost infinitely so because there are always players finding new ways to use it, and also because it often gets updated when Minecraft itself gets an update. This book is not meant to contain every single piece of information about Redstone, as that would be impossible, at the worst, or require a book that was a few thousand pages longer at best.

What this book is meant to do is to give you all of the basic information you need to begin learning how to use Redstone in the easiest and most pain free way we can teach it to you. We want to make Redstone fun and inviting, and to dispel the air of intimidation and difficulty that often surrounds the subject.

We'll take you from the very most basic concepts of Redstone, starting here in this chapter, and as we go through the book, we'll add a little more with each chapter, stopping along the way to test out the ideas we present with some fun builds and cool applications.

We suggest that you approach this book from one end to the other, working through each chapter in turn and learning its lessons before moving on to the next. By the end of the book, we'll have you building some pretty highly advanced Redstone constructions and starting to think like a real Redstone engineer!

That being said, these concepts are also very complex, and there's a lot of information to internalize, so we'd also make one more suggestion for how to have the best and most successful Redstone learning experience:

Don't worry about getting it all perfect. Even the best Redstone engineers out there took a long time to understand and memorize this information, and there's no rush to do so. The best way to learn Redstone is to read through this book and test out the different builds, and then to just keep messing around with the stuff, referring back to the book when you need to know something. Over time, you'll start to naturally remember the nitty gritty details of Redstone items, rules and concepts without having to look them up, so there's no need to get discouraged if you keep having to look back at the book as you go.

In fact, we'd even suggest seeking out more resources on Redstone as well, such as watching videos online or finding other players to learn from. This book is meant to be your introduction to the world of Redstone and a handy reference guide, but we won't have our feelings hurt if you need to seek out a little extra help! The goal here is to help you learn Redstone, and we are simply trying give you as many resources in these pages as possible to help you do that.

One final note before we get going: Almost everything we talk about in this book assumes that you are playing in Creative Mode. This is because the builds take very, very many items of different types, and while you might have them in your Survival World, they will be pretty expensive. Additionally, Creative Mode allows you to fly and to turn off hostile mobs, allowing you to be able to learn in peace. We can't suggest doing this enough to learn Redstone's rules. Additionally, this book is primarily focused on the full version of Minecraft as it is on the PC and Mac. This is because the console versions do not contain all Redstone items quite yet, but they are being updated frequently. If you are playing on a console, you'll have to wait to try some of these concepts until the updates happen, but the basic rules and many of the builds are still the same and will work.

**With that in mind, let's get into this!**

# The Concept

In a nutshell, Redstone is a system that uses power signals to cause something to happen in the game of Minecraft. This "something" could be as simple as opening a Door or turning on a light, or it could be something a bit more complex like causing a mechanism such as a Piston to activate and interact with the world, or it could be as complex as causing a mini-game to begin. A simple Redstone power signal can even cause something as intricate and massive as a player-built Redstone simulation of a computer to turn on and function!

Redstone power is somewhat like real-life electricity, and thinking of it like this is very useful, especially when first starting out with the stuff. Here are the ways in which Redstone and real-world electricity are similar:

- **Redstone has an ON state and an OFF state.**

- **Redstone signals can have various levels of power, in the case of Redstone it goes from 0-15.**

- **Redstone signals can be carried through a Minecraft world through items called Redstone Dust (as well as others) that are very similar to real-life wires.**

- **A powered Redstone signal that is "wired" up so that it runs into certain items in the game called "mechanisms" will give those mechanisms power and cause them to activate.**

- **Redstone can be used to build "circuits" that function in much the same way as real-life circuits function in computers and other electronics.**

There are, however, quite a few ways in which Redstone and normal electricity differ, and they are equally important:

**The power that Redstone builds** use is not always held in a storage unit like a battery, or piped through from the outside, but is instead almost always created by the items that toggle the power ON and OFF. To further explain the difference, a real-world light switch controls electric power, but it does not create the power. In Minecraft, Levers, which are very similar in look to light-switches, can control Redstone power, but they also create that power themselves. Redstone items that create power are called "power components," and there are many types of these, including two that do act somewhat like a battery and/or permanent power source (Redstone Torches and Blocks of Redstone).

**Redstone power signals only go 15 blocks** in one direction before their power signal fades away. To get it to go farther, it must be boosted. This is actually similar to real electricity, except that the rules that govern the distance of real electric signals are far more complex.

**Redstone signals can and often are influenced by the passage of time.** This is also actually similar to real electricity, but again there is a major difference. This time the difference is that the time delays on real electricity are often so fast that we do not even recognize them, while in Redstone this is essentially slowed way down so that players can manipulate and use these delays. Time in Redstone is measured in "ticks," where each a tick happens 10 times a second, or once every 0.1 seconds in real time. Redstone components and mechanisms update their status every tick, checking to see if their inputs have changed in any way, and when the input does change, they respond by activating, deactivating or performing a special action. Note: time in the rest of Minecraft also operates on "ticks," but a regular Minecraft ticks happen 20 times a second, making them twice as fast. This often confuses players who are aware of regular Minecraft ticks, so it's a good idea to note the difference here. Additionally, when we refer to "ticks" from here on out in this book, we are referring exclusively to Redstone ticks.

When you know how to use these and the many other rules of Redstone together, you will be able to build incredible contraptions and systems, and the range of things you can do in everyone's favorite builder game expands in a huge way. In fact, Redstone is considered by many players to be the pinnacle of Minecraft knowledge, and many of the things that people build in the game that will cause less-experienced players to scratch their head and wonder how it even happened are made with Redstone.

# The Components

Redstone is possible because of certain items and blocks in the game and the way they work together. In the next chapter, we'll look at each and every one of these very closely and give you all the details of how they work and what they're used in, but for now let's break the various Redstone components down into their most simple forms and talk about how they relate.

All Redstone items fall into one of the following categories:

1. **Power & control components (usually just referred to as power components)**
2. **Transmission components**
3. **Mechanisms**
4. **Basic blocks**
5. **Rails and Rail-related items**
6. **Other items that interact with Redstone**

In its most simple form, a Redstone build will have a power component and a mechanism, but most Redstone builds use items from at least three of these categories, and some can even use many items from all of these categories.

Let's take a second to get the basics of how the first three of these components interact with each other set in our minds. A typical simple Redstone build starts with a power component, which sends a power signal out. This is often carried by transmission components to either other Redstone circuits or to mechanisms. When mechanisms receive an ON power signal, they activate.

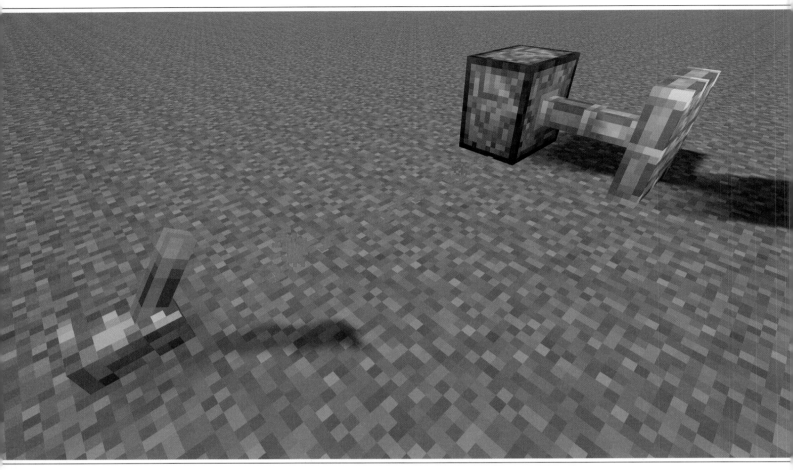

This is the basic Redstone setup: power component, wire and mechanism.

Somewhere in this process of sending a power signal from power component>transmission component>mechanism, the signal may interact with basic blocks of the game. What we mean by this is blocks that are usually used for building purposes, such as Cobblestone, Dirt, Wool, Glass, etc. There are two important types of blocks when it comes to Redstone, and they interact with Redstone in different ways:

**Opaque blocks:** "Opaque" is a word that means an object through which light does not travel. In Minecraft, this definition usually applies as well. Opaque blocks are important to Redstone because they can be powered by a Redstone signal. When a block is "powered," this means that a Redstone signal is going into it, and that Redstone mechanisms, as well as Repeaters and Comparators (more on these in the Items chapter), will be activated by the block. This property of allowing Redstone signals to travel through themselves makes opaque blocks very important to Redstone.

**Transparent blocks:** As you might guess "transparent" blocks are typically those that can be "seen through" in the game, though this term also refers to a few such as Glowstone and Slabs that the game merely treats as transparent, though they themselves block vision. In terms of Redstone, transparent blocks are important because they do not take a Redstone power signal, even if one is going straight into them. This makes transparent blocks very useful to separate and block currents in Redstone building.

Our final two types of Redstone items (Rail items, and other interactable blocks) are not nearly as core to

Some transparent blocks (left) and some opaque blocks (right).

Redstone concepts and building as the first four, though they can be integral parts of specific Redstone builds. These are essentially specialty items that can be used to create very specific results, as opposed to items that you'll be using in every build. More on these in the next chapter; all you really need to do now is to be aware that Rails and rail-related items as well as a few unique items can also interact with Redstone builds.

## Putting it All Together for the First Time

Okay! So we know a bit about what Redstone is, we know a few of its rules, and we know the basic types of items that are used in Redstone builds, so it's time to actually test the stuff out!

We'll wrap this first chapter up by doing some small Redstone placement, and talk a bit about what's happening with each thing we do. Open up your Minecraft, get a new world started in Creative Mode, and let's play with a little Redstone.

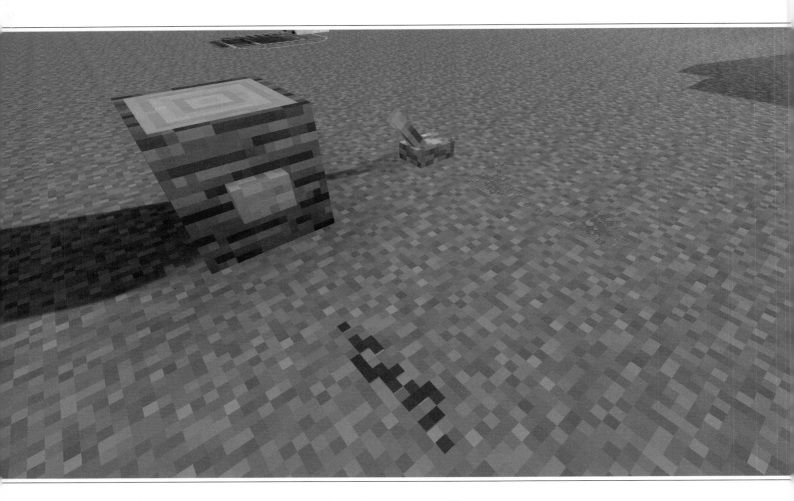

# 1. Component + Redstone Dust

First thing's first: let's see some Redstone actually powered up. Put a Lever, a Button (either kind) and some Redstone into your inventory. Place the Lever on the ground, and then place Redstone Dust on the ground right next to it. Now scoot over a bit and place the Button on a block (any opaque block is fine) and place Redstone Dust on the ground right in front of this. Make sure this second Dust is not touching the first and is not adjacent to the Lever. Now, activate the Lever. See how the Redstone Dust lights up when you flick the Lever? This means it's powered, and that the power state is constant. If you want to turn it OFF, just flip the Lever to the other state. Now press the Button. See the difference? For the Button, the Redstone was only powered for a brief moment, and then it went off. This example is just to show you how Redstone Dust can be powered, and that different power components power it differently (in this case a constant signal vs. a temporary one).

## 2. Trying A Mechanism

Now flip your Lever OFF, and then put a Piston into your inventory. Place the Piston down adjacent to the Redstone Dust you placed next to your Lever, and then flip the Lever ON. As you can see, as soon as you flip the Lever, the Piston will activate, extending. This is the simplest form of a Redstone build (perhaps your first ever!). All that's happening here is that the Lever is providing a signal, the Dust is carrying the signal to the Piston, and the Piston is recognizing that it is powered and is firing. Though most Redstone builds get much more complicated than this, essentially this is what is happening at the basic level in almost all Redstone creations.

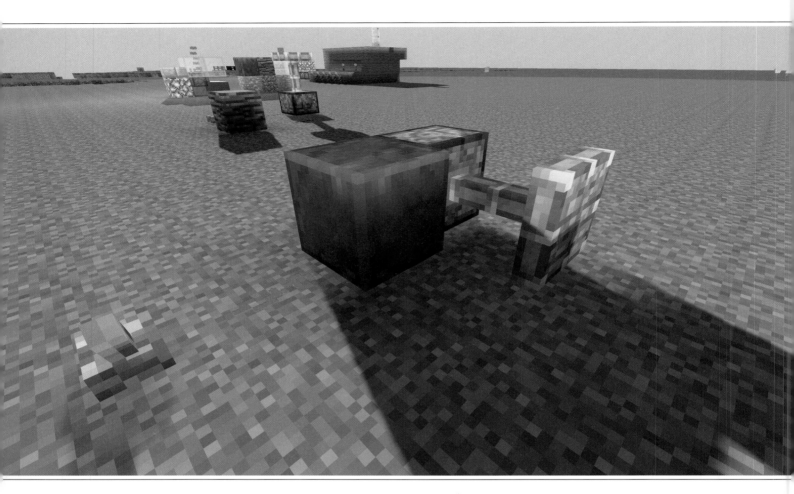

# 3. Powering An Opaque Block

Next, get a second Piston in your inventory, as well as a Redstone Torch and an opaque block. Move away from the Redstone items you have already placed, and put the opaque block down on the ground. Place a dot of Redstone Dust on the ground adjacent to the block (not on top of it though, for now), and then place the Redstone Torch on the opposite side of this Dust from the block. Now, go around to the opposite side of the block, and place the Piston down adjacent to this side of the block so that it is touching the block. For this example, make sure that the Piston is not adjacent to the Dust. You'll notice that the Piston also fires in this situation. This is because the block it is on is now "powered," which we talked about earlier in this chapter. The Redstone Torch, in this case, is providing the power signal to the Dust, which goes into the block and powers it, which then transfers the power to the mechanism. In this way we can see how powering blocks works and can be useful in Redstone.

# 4. Making Things More Complex With A Repeater

We're going to look at a very basic example of how we can make a Redstone build more complex for our final example. We'll need another Piston, another Lever and a Redstone Repeater for this one. Move away from your other Redstone builds, and place your Lever down on the ground. Put one dot of Redstone Dust adjacent to this Lever, and then stand on that Dust so that you are facing the opposite direction of the Lever. Aim down at the block on the opposite side of the Dust from the Lever while still standing on the Dust, and place your Repeater down. Now place the Piston on the block just after the Repeater, so you have a line of items that goes Lever>Dust>Repeater>Piston. Now flip the Lever. As you'll see, the Redstone current will go through the Dust, hit the Repeater, and then a slight amount of time later the Piston will fire. One of the features of Repeaters is that they output a signal at a slight delay, which in this case causes the Piston to fire, but which also has many other uses. We'll get to those later, but for now just notice how we can make the standard Redstone configuration more complex with other items.

**Alrighty, we've done a little Redstone! That wasn't so bad, was it? Now you've got a bit of experience with the stuff, are starting to understand how it works, and hey! You can even tell your friends that you've started using Redstone. Good job miner!**

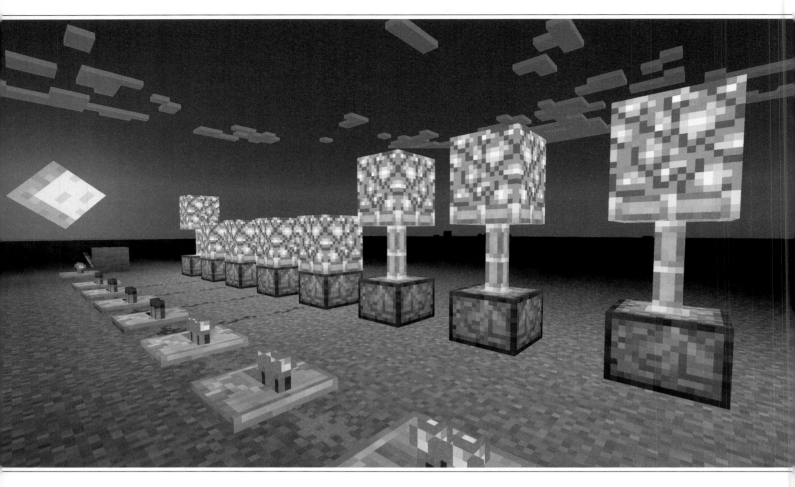

# Your First 4 Redstone Builds

All this talk about the components and concepts and rules of Redstone has probably got you a bit overwhelmed, but don't worry: actually doing a little Redstone will help you tremendously in figuring out just what all that information means, as well as how to use it to make Minecraft even more awesome than it already is. So, young crafters, here's the part where we stop just telling you about Redstone and start actually makin' some cool stuff! These are your first five true Redstone builds, starting from the simplest Redstone doorbell and going through an awesome-lookin' Piston wave that's a great and easy way to impress those who don't have your Redstone skills.

So, young crafters, here's the part where we stop just telling you about Redstone and start actually makin' some cool stuff! These are your first five true Redstone builds, starting from the simplest Redstone doorbell and going through an awesome-lookin' Piston wave that's a great and easy way to impress those who don't have your Redstone skills.

These builds are designed to be super simple to build, in order to get you comfortable with using Redstone, yet they'll also teach you important lessons about Redstone and its properties. The builds also incorporate a few more complex properties and functions of Redstone, such as a NOT Gate and a clock, which you'll become much more familiar with later in the book as we get into more complex and difficult Redstone builds.

For now, however, we just want to focus on building the five contraptions here and understanding the simple basics of how they work. Later, we'll get into the more complex ideas behind some of the functions in these builds, but this chapter is all about dipping your toes into the world of Redstone in the simplest, most pain-free way possible. All you've got to do is follow the instructions and then recreate what you see in the images, and you'll already be on your way to earning your honorary Master's degree in Redstone Engineering.

*Note:* We recommend doing this in Creative Mode in order to learn these builds, but you can do them in Survival Mode as well if you have the materials.

## The Doorbell

**What it does:** Lets ya know someone wants in your house by making a ding (or y'know, whatever weird noise you set it to).

**How it works:** A Note Block inside your home makes a noise when someone outside pushes a Button, powering the Note Block.

**You'll Need:** 1 Button, 1 Note Block, Redstone (optional)

Makin' a working, useful doorbell is just about the easiest Redstone project you'll ever do. In fact, it can be done without any Redstone Wire at all if you don't mind the Note Block being right inside your door. This is a good project to just get an idea of how power-giving items such as

Buttons work with items like the Note Block that take power, and it's a cute little way to spruce up your home. Plus, Note Blocks can be heard up to 48 blocks from its location, so it will inform you of visitors even at a good distance.

**1. Find the spot** where you'd like to put the button that will activate your doorbell. Typically these are placed by a Door, but you could do it anywhere you wanted. For the easiest Doorbell, pick a spot on a wall near a Door that is one block off the ground and where the wall is just one block thick behind where the Button will be. Place the Button on this block.

**2. Place the Note Block** on the other side of the block that now has a Button on it.

**3. If the block under the Note Block** is one you placed yourself, break it and leave the space empty. If you can't remember if you placed the block then go ahead and break it. This is done because the Note Block will change to a different sound than the beep we want if a human-placed block is underneath it.

**4. Right-click the Note Block** until it hits the note you'd like to use as your doorbell. This can be a little tricky, as sometimes the Note Block doesn't want to make noise, but just break the block and put it back down if you can't get it to work at first.

**5. Press the Button** back on the other side of the wall, and the Note Block will make its sound! The way this works is that the Button gives power to the block it is placed on, and this block gives power to the Note Block.

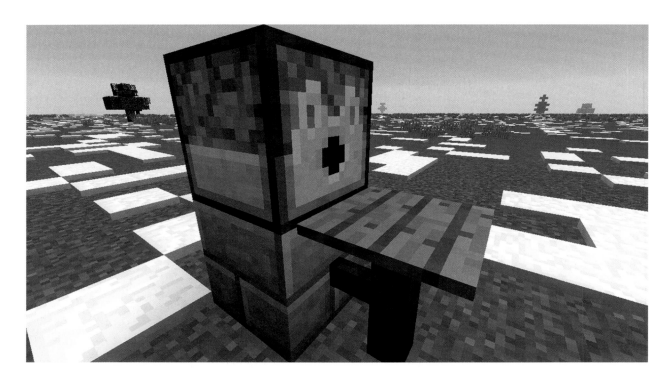

# The Easy Potion Dispenser

**What it does:** Throws a Potion out at you when you run up and bump it (no need to click on this one).

**How it works:** A Dispenser is placed on a block, a Fence is placed in front of the block and Dispenser, and on top of the Fence is a Pressure Plate. When you run up to the Pressure Plate and push your crafter into it, it will press down, and whatever is in the Dispenser will launch out (Potions, in this case)

**You'll Need:** 1 Dispenser, 1 Fence, 1 Pressure Plate, 1 random block (optional, Dispenser could hang in the air), whatever Potions you want to dispense

Another quite simple little doohickey, the easy Potion dispenser makes taking Potions in Minecraft about as easy as it can be. Typically, you have to open your inventory or go to your hot bar and actually use a potion, or even run up to a Dispenser and push a Button or pull a Lever to get one to launch out at you. However, with the Easy Potion Dispenser, all you have to do is run up and bump the Pressure Plate, and you'll be smartly splashed with Potion.

**1. Place a block** of any kind down.

**2. Put a Dispenser** on top of this block.

**3. Fill the Dispenser** with a Potion of your choosing. This will actually work with anything a Dispenser can dispense at you, but Potions are one of the most useful options in this configuration.

**4. Stand so the Dispenser** is facing you (the side with the O-shaped hole) and look down at the block it is sitting on. Place one Fence on the block that is in front of this block that the Dispenser is on.

**5. Place a Pressure Plate** on top of the one Fence you have just placed.

**6. Run up to the Pressure Plate,** and it will press down and the Potion (or whatever else you've got in the Dispenser) will launch out. This is the Pressure Plate activating from interacting with your body and powering the Dispenser, which fires a random item inside of it at you.

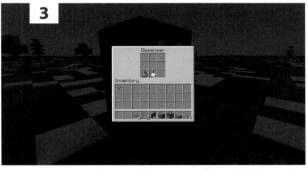

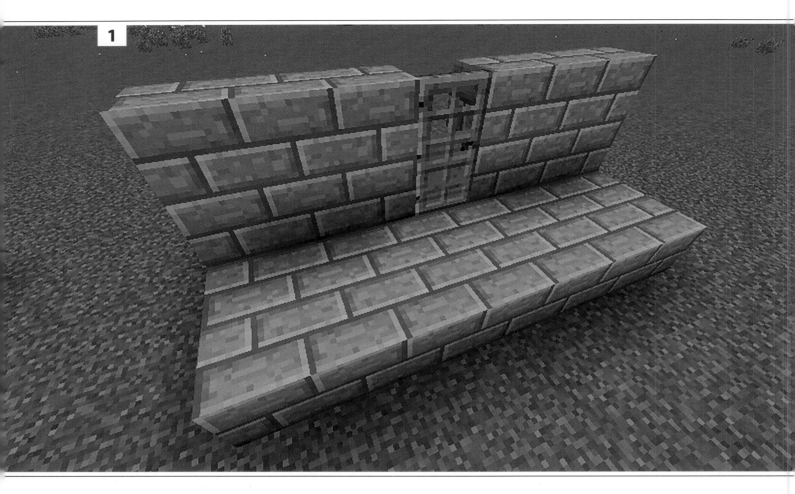

# The Trapdoor

**What it does:** Opens a hole in the ground wherever you'd like (in this case in front of a Door) at the flick of a Lever. Beneath this hole that opens is a big pit and/or Lava, which anything that was standing on the block above the hole will fall into.

**How it works:** A Sticky Piston is attached to a block and extended over a pit, covering the hole. The Sticky Piston is attached underground to a Redstone "gate" called a Not Gate (look to the Gates chapter for further explanation of this), which goes beneath the wall of a house using Redstone Wire. On the other side of the wall,

a Lever on the ground surface turns the signal for the Redstone wire on and off, causing the Sticky Piston to expose and to cover the pit, alternatively. The whole contraption is hidden.

**You'll Need:** 1 Sticky Piston, 1 Lever, 1 Redstone Torch, 2 Redstone Wire, 2 Slabs of any kind, 1 random block

**1. Find yourself a nice Door.** This Door should be one which you would like to look out of, see a Creeper, and then kill that Creeper by making it drop to its doom. Also works with annoying players.

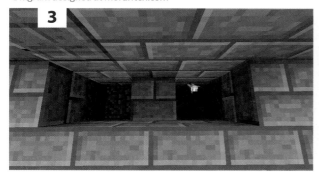

Diagram designed at mordritch.com

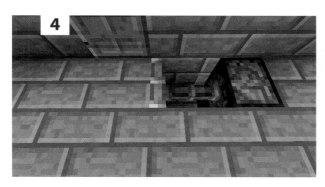

**2. Dig out a pit** in the pattern of Diagram 1. It should be only 1 block wide and 3 long, and it should alternate being 2 and 1 and then 2 blocks deep, as you also see in the Diagram.

**3. Place a Redstone Torch** on the wall as you see in the photo here.

**4. Put a Sticky Piston** in the space above the Redstone Torch facing toward the space in front of the Door (it will extend automatically), and then put a block of whatever type you'd like in front of the Sticky Piston. The 1 block deep hole in front of the Door should now be covered by the block stuck to the Sticky Piston.

**5. Go to the other side** of the wall which the Door is set in. Dig out a pit immediately on the other side of the wall from the block where the Sticky Piston and Redstone Torch are. Make this pit 1 block wide, 2 blocks long and 2 blocks deep, as in the picture.

**6. Lay Redstone Wire down** on the bottom of this pit. This is not essential to understand at this point, but what you have created in this section of the build is represented in Diagram 2.

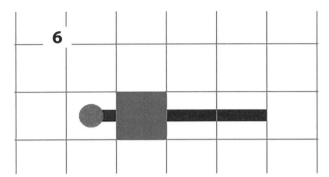

Diagram designed at mordritch.com

By adding a power source to the end of the Redstone Wire in Diagram 2 (or on a block above it, as we will do in the next step), we create what is called a NOT Gate. A NOT Gate is a type of construction known as a logic gate, which manipulates a Redstone signal and is something we will learn in the future chapter on Gates.

**7. Cover the last block** of the pit (farthest from the wall) with the same type of block that makes up the rest of the floor. Put a Lever on top of this block. Now cover the second block of the pit with the same type of block, but with no Lever.

**8. Flip the Lever** and the Sticky Piston should pull back and uncover the hole in front of the Door.

**9. Go back through the Door** to the pit in front of it, and dig the pit deeper. Here you have a few options: place Lava or Cactus at the bottom of the pit to kill intruders with damage, make a long drop that will kill the intruder (at least 24 blocks down for a TKO), or build an area at the bottom for the intruders to fall into and just, y'know, hang out. Until you come to slice them up with your Sword, of course.

**10. Go back up** and cover up the Sticky Piston by placing 2 Slabs of any kind on top of the two blocks it takes up. Don't put one over the spot in front of the door, of course.

**11. Wait for a Creeper** to come stand outside your door, flip the Lever, profit.

# The Simplest Clock

**What it does:** Creates a pulse of Redstone power that turns on and off at a regular interval, which allows many concepts to be created with Redstone, including but not limited to contraptions that keep time.

**How it works:** A Redstone Torch powers a Redstone Repeater, which slows down the signal slightly (in this case it is a '4 tick' delay). After 4 ticks the power goes through the Repeater and on to the Wire after it, which curves around to power the block that the original Redstone Torch was on. This turns off the Redstone Torch

temporarily, in turn turning off the signal through the Redstone Repeater after 4 more ticks. This repeats indefinitely unless acted upon from an outside signal.

**You'll Need:** 1 Redstone Torch, 1 Redstone Repeater, 3 Redstone Wire, 1 Random Block

When referring to Redstone components, a "clock" is a Redstone construction that alternately causes an on signal and then an off signal to be transmitted from itself every so many seconds in a constant pulse.

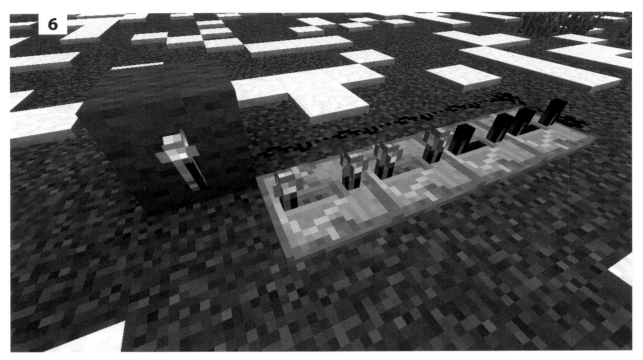

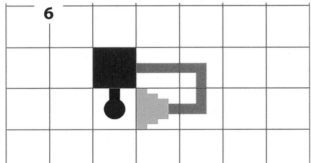

Diagram designed at mordritch.com

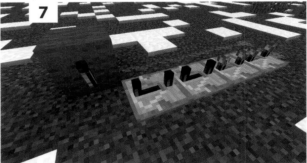

Clocks are power loops, where a signal is transmitted from a power source, slowed down by Repeaters (or other ways, in more complex cases), and then is sent back to the original power source, temporarily turning it off. This causes the power to pulse with a consistent amount of time between each pulse, and the amount of time between each pulse can be customized by the builder through using multiple Repeaters in a row as well as other tactics.

This pulsing signal can be used to give something else power for a few ticks, and then take it away.

So for instance, a Piston hooked up to a clock would continuously extend and pull back as long as it was hooked up to the clock.

This is the simplest version of a clock, and it's quite useful for everything from practical, mechanical Redstone builds to the most complex logic circuits.

**1. Turn so that the direction** you would like your power to go in is to your right. Make sure there are about five blocks of usable ground space to your right (if there is not, scooch over a bit so there is).

**2. Place your random block down.** This has to be one that can transfer power, so something like Stone, Wool or Wood of any type is good.

**3. Keeping the direction** you would like the signal to move in to your right, place a Redstone Torch on the side of the block facing you, as in the image.

**4. As in the image,** place a Redstone Repeater on the block to the right of the block that your Redstone Torch hangs over (so, caddy-corner to the block the Redstone Torch is on).

**5. Set this repeater** on the last setting (4 ticks). This is important- Redstone Torches cannot take a signal that is too fast coming back into them, and Redstone Torches will burn out after a while if you have too quick of a signal piping into them (turn your Repeater to a faster signal when your

clock is fully built and test it out sometime, just to see this happen). The reason for this is somewhat complex, but all you need to know at this point is that you need to slow this signal down a bit with your Repeater.

**6. Copy the Redstone pattern** from the Diagram, taking it one block on the ground past the repeater, then both blocks on the ground to the right of the block you have a Torch on.

**7. If you have set the Repeater** to the right delay in step #5, your clock will start working immediately, doing a pulsing signal.

**8. To use your clock,** just put 1 Redstone Wire branching off of the existing Redstone Wire in the clock. You can then extend this to whatever you want to power.

# Tips:

You can put a Lever on the side of the block in your Redstone clock, and you can turn the clock on and off with the Lever.

You can create clocks with greater delays (much greater, theoretically) by using more Redstone Repeaters in a row.